PURIFY
THIS HOUSE

CHALLENGES AND TRIUMPHS
OF BLENDED FAMILIES

ALTHEA P. JONES

Published by Victorious You Press™

Printed in the United States of America

ISBN: 978-1-952756-49-8

For details email vyp.joantrandall@gmail.com

or visit us at www.victoriousyoupress.com

ACKNOWLEDGMENTS

I give thanks and honor to the Author and Finisher of my faith, my Heavenly Father, who has given me the gift of writing. "My heart is full of beautiful words as I say my poem for the king. My tongue is like the pen of a skillful writer" Psalms 45:1 (New International Reader's Version).

Acknowledgments go out to every parent who has done their best to raise their children with the skills they have learned and with love by tapping into their mind, body, and spirit.

I acknowledge the great men and women who have impacted my life whose shoulders I stand on: To Willie L. Jones, my dear loving, supportive husband who continuously encouraged me along this journey. You are an amazing man, and God knew I needed you as my leader.

To my role model, Clara J. Bright, my sweet mother, God chose you to carry me for nine months. I gained so much wisdom and strength from you. You have always been my cheerleader. Thank you for leading me to Christ! To my dear father, Oliver L. Jasper Sr. Through your love for your family, you taught me the importance of being committed to family life.

Also, your love for gardening put food on our table. In turn, you taught me how to garden. Now, I can provide fresh produce for my family.

God knew the mission he had given me would require more special people to help guide me. So, thank you, Gussie L. Jasper (stepmother), for the many jewels you taught me in life, especially how to endure when life throws unexpected turns. Philip Bright (stepfather), thank you for being a student of life. You did not mind sharing your wisdom. I shall never forget you teaching me the importance and benefits of being responsible. This knowledge has taken me far in life.

Alma L. Gillespie, who I lovingly called Mama G., a nickname I gave her. I am so thankful you were not the typical "Mother-in-law" as often depicted in the world. You were a breath of fresh air that blew calmly when we were together. I applaud you for what you instilled in your son to be the best man he could be. May you rest in peace.

A special thanks to each of my wonderful siblings, Lynda (Gerald); Oliver Jr. (Sadie); Connie (Nathan); Ronald, Jeffrey, Jeanette, Patricia, Loretta, and Gwendolyn. I love you all for sharing a piece of yourselves with me, which helped me to become the person I am today.

To my awesome children, The Player J's– Donald, Steffon, Shambé, Marcus Jones, and Nicole Crowley (Channon). You have often been my strength. For that, I am very appreciative and thankful.

To my Godchildren, Mauricus Brooks, Shontrell Jasper, Carolyn Rucker, A. J. Jackson, William Phelps III, Merriella Phelps, Jourdian Stewart, Semaj Bostic, and Tracy Jasper. Having you in my life allowed the sun to shine even brighter.

To all my Grandchildren and Great-grandchildren, I am so very blessed to have each of you in my life. I pray I will live to see you all become wonderful, God-fearing adults. You are well on your way and keep up God's work.

To my dear in-laws and close friends who have inspired me in so many ways, from the east coast to the west coast, north, and south, I salute you.

A midwife is known as a specialized health professional who cares for mothers and newborns. Joan T. Randall, my publisher at Victorious You Press, was my personal manuscript midwife as I labored for more than nine months. Now that my contractions are over, I can breathe. Thank you and all the staff at Victorious You Press for helping me bring this manuscript to print.

To Lynn Braxton, my Editor. I thank God for you enriching my life in so many ways. Thank you for the encouragement, the prayers, and thoughtfulness on many projects you helped birth. Words cannot express my gratitude.

To my silent mentors, I appreciate you passing the torch to those of us who are thirsty for living and learning: Althea Gibson (my namesake), Sojourner Truth, Martin Luther King Jr., Harriett, Tubman, Maya Angelou, T.D., and Serita Jakes,

Oprah Winfrey, former President Barak Obama, and former First Lady Michelle Obama. I love you all because you paved the way for so many people.

As I continue on this journey, I recognize that God is not through with me yet!

"Communication is the ability to ensure that people understand not only what you say but also what you mean. It is also the ability to listen to and understand others. Developing both aspects of communication takes a lot of time, patience, and hard work." **~Myles Munroe~**

TABLE OF CONTENTS

WE ARE A BLENDED FAMILY
My children-Your children-Our children

We are blended.

Your daddy loves my mommy!

And my mommy loves your daddy,

That makes him my poppy, too.

Get married is what they are going to do.

We are blended.

The two of them make a pair.

But I thought you lived over there.

Now you live with us.

Do not worry we will not make a fuss.

We are blended.

More people to love, and more to love you.

There's so much we can do.

We are a loving and caring family,

With deep roots like a tree.

We are blended.

No longer broken, together we are mended

Oh, I get it.

Blended like a puzzle, we make a perfect fit!

By Althea P. Jones

1

INTRODUCTION

❦

"**N**o! You will not date while living in this house!" Daddy Matthews said as he pounded on the table.

"I know this is not what you want, but this is what I want! I am old enough to do what I want," Sissy snapped back.

Daddy Matthews yelled, "Who do you think you are? I *said,* as long as you live in my house, you will do as I say, or else you can..."

Mama Hannah came rushing into the room, jumped between Sissy and Daddy Matthews, trying to stop the chaos. "What is going on?" She did not want to take sides; she just wanted the screaming to stop. What she was hoping for, did not turn out like she thought it would. Daddy Matthews was furious. Sissy was angry and stormed out of the house.

A GLIMPSE INTO A DYSFUNCTIONAL BLENDED FAMILY

This story is a snapshot into the life of a dysfunctional blended family. It is not the expected outcome for all blended families. However, members of this type of family may end up in future toxic relationships. They are busy trying to please themselves or others and are not concerned whether their actions are appropriate or not. Other family members only care about themselves and do not care about anyone else's feelings. The parents are often modeling what they observed their parents do. Later in life, when the children become adults, they will have boyfriends or girlfriends, husbands, or wives, and act out what they believe relationships should look like based on what they observed as kids. It becomes a vicious cycle if no one breaks it.

In the dysfunctional blended families in this story, women were the caregivers who gave a lot of themselves but did not receive much in return. When they became fed up, they spoke up and reacted from a place of hurt and anger. The men were the authority figures, and when rules were overlooked or broken,

5

they would overreact because they were operating from a place of brokenness–by lashing out at family members. This behavior usually brought out negative reactions from the person being attacked. When people feel they are undervalued, they tend to exhibit negative behaviors. In these families, feelings are commonly not expressed appropriately.

It is possible for a dysfunctional family to become functional, but they need to put God first, surrender to Him, ask forgiveness for past sins, and ask God for help. These are the steps towards becoming "functional." The pain that is caused in dysfunctional families is usually long-lasting if not dealt with properly and in a timely fashion. Repairing the brokenness in dysfunctional families is possible! Only God can break the yoke of the past.

Chapter 1
Chaos in the Family

"This is getting way too difficult for me, with no help from you!" Hannah sighed. "Bubba, are you listening to me?" She continued, "I need you to come home after you get off work to help with the children. I did not sign up to do this all by myself!" Hannah was irritated that Bubba had not responded to her concerns. She looked back and saw him lying in bed with his hands behind his head, fast asleep. "Bubba," she shouted.

Suddenly, Bubba got up, grabbed the glass off the nightstand, and threw it across the room–hitting the wall. This is how he often displayed his anger or frustration. The sound of the glass shattering startled Hannah–she jumped. She knew cleaning up the broken pieces was an added chore along with all her regular chores. Bubba did not do any chores around the house.

Despite his negative actions, their marriage started out like most. Bubba and Hannah were both young when they got married. They had their first child when Hannah was in her early twenties. She was pregnant every year for the next years. Sissy was the oldest; Big Bro came after Sissy; Jacob was next, and Lillie was the youngest. Even though Hannah and Bubba had four children, neither was sure if they really wanted that many so soon.

Bubba left his parent's home when he was a young teen, so he did not get all the training he needed to become a responsible man. Being a provider was one of his strongest qualities. He provided the essentials for their family. He was a hardworking man, but he played as hard as he worked, if not harder. He put his social life before his family. When Hannah needed companionship and help with the children, he was gone. Life became extremely difficult. Being married became a chore, along with working, keeping the home together, and taking care of a growing family. Bubba drank his sorrows away, leaving Hannah to cry herself to sleep night after night.

The next evening, Bubba did not come home as Hannah had asked. She waited up in hopes that he would. She asked him questions about his whereabouts–which made him really upset. The questions usually came when he was drunk, and he did not want to talk. The morning after, while he was getting ready for work, he continued to be silent. That type of behavior left Hannah confused. She could see they were slowly drifting apart. He had a reason for being gone eight hours a day. But after work, he had no acceptable excuses. Usually, he was gone for another seven or eight hours. Communication is supposed to be a very key part of any relationship, but Hannah recognized that it was not the case in their marriage.

Hannah could not understand how Bubba would be so drunk, come home so late, then get up the next morning and get ready for work as if nothing happened. Her thoughts were not healthy. She paced back and forth most nights, thinking about what Bubba might be doing and if she should leave or not. The thought of taking the children was one that kept her from going. Both physically and mentally, Hannah knew she was not prepared to take them. She agonized deeply over whether to stay or go. She did not know anyone who would allow her and her babies to live with them.

"Bubba, I have been trying to talk to you for some time now. But you seem to be too busy having fun. You pay no attention to what I have to say," she said softly. Every night I pace the floor, praying that you will make it home safely. I have been hoping to talk to you about what I have been feeling. But when you don't come home, I cry myself to sleep. Bubba, it has caught up with us. I can't do this by myself anymore," she said, turning her back to him to hide her tears.

In her heart, Hannah would rather have talked to Bubba about fixing what was broken in their relationship when he was sober. He had pushed her to her limit. As she was talking, Hannah heard a thump. Bubba had fallen onto the bed in the middle of Hannah's conversation. He was drunk and sound asleep. Hannah did not want to make any decisions while she was feeling distraught. She needed to do something before someone got hurt. But whatever she decided, she knew it would impact her and her family.

Hannah walked towards the closet to get her things. With tears streaming down her face, she cried out from deep within her soul, "Bubba, I do not want to do this, but you leave me no choice. I really want to take my babies with me! I do not want to leave them here with you! But no one has room for all of us," she said and threw her hands in the air. Bubba did not hear any of Hannah's conversation. He was sound asleep and snoring.

Hannah knelt down in the closet and pushed the blankets aside to retrieve her suitcase. She pulled it out and placed it on the floor beside her. She brushed her hands across it as she re-called that this was the same suitcase she had when she and Bubba got married and moved into their first home together. As she opened it, she broke down crying again, because she could not believe what was happening. The last time Hannah unpacked this suitcase, she was very much in love with Bubba.

Hannah pulled her few pieces of clothing off the hangers and placed them in the suitcase. She only owned a few items, so there wasn't much to pack. She was so distraught, *"What am I going to do? I am so tired of this! I just cannot do this any-more!"*

When she finally pulled herself together, she wiped the tears away, straightened her shoulders, held her head up high, and walked over to the dresser, and pulled open the two drawers where the last of her belongings were. Hannah placed them in her suitcase and gently closed it. Glancing around the room, she wanted to make sure she had everything. Then she looked at her hand, remembering she still had her wedding ring on. Slowly removing her ring, she said softly, "For better or for worse, huh?" She shook her head and put the ring on the dresser, and walked out of the room.

Hannah went into the boys' and girls' bedrooms and kissed them goodbye. As she was walking down the hall one last time, she stopped at her bedroom door and peered at Bubba, still in a drunken stupor and sound asleep.

CHAPTER 2
FAITH WALK

With her suitcase in her hand, Hannah walked out the front door, closing it quietly behind her. She stood on the porch and looked in both directions trying to figure out which way to go. As she stepped off the porch and descended down the steps, she burst into tears. *"How can I leave my babies behind?"* It was pitch black–she felt all alone. Fear seemed to overwhelm her when she reached the bottom of the stairs. Hannah knew all along what had stopped her from leaving in the past; it was fear. So, she took a deep breath, and with a leap of faith, she took the first step. As she continued walking down the sidewalk, the steps became easier and easier. The further she walked, the braver she became, even though she had no idea where she was headed.

Hannah had been walking for some time, and her suitcase was getting heavy. The night grew quieter, and her steps slowed down, so did her breathing. Hannah could see the light shining through the windows of the train station in the distance. When she reached the door, she pulled on the handle and went inside. No one was in sight, so she sat in the seat farthest away from the

13

ticket counter because she did not want to draw attention to herself. Exhaustion overcame her as she sat down on the bench. She put her suitcase next to her. Hannah could not fall asleep because of the chill in the air. So, she covered her legs and arms with her jacket to keep warm. She closed her eyes and leaned back against the headrest. Her head bobbed back and forth, and soon she was sound asleep.

Hannah began to have an unusual dream. She did not know that God had intentionally put her in a deep sleep so he could have this uninterrupted time with her.

"I heard about You, God, but I never felt worthy or that I would need to talk to you this soon. I also heard others say you hear them when they pray, so I want you to hear me because this is really, really important. Okay? Are you listening to me, God? Well, I am going to keep talking until I hear you say something, anything. I know I am at a breaking point in my relationship with Bubba. I am scared and nervous. We both are confused. Being in this state of confusion is causing me not to behave like myself. Therefore, I am not the wife and mother I need to be. I have been trying to talk to Bubba before we got to this point, but he refused to take me seriously. God, people have told me you have all the answers; therefore, I am talking to you.

When I married, I made up my mind to follow my vows. I do not want to leave Bubba. When we married, we vowed to honor you most of all. Now that I have left him, you may be mad at me. Is that why you are not saying anything? God, I need you to show me, tell me what to do. When Bubba and I try to talk, either we get into a big argument, or he will not talk. He blames me, and I blame him. He thinks he is right, and I think I am right too. Another thing that hurts so bad, Bubba comes home drunk almost every night. Earlier in our marriage, he was not drinking as much. We were getting along just fine. I think if he did not drink, he would be a great guy for my babies and me. I guess when our family grew, it may have driven him to drink. Drinking to bury his problems is not the answer. I do not want to hide my problems from you! I need your help!" she stated.

In her dream, God showed Hannah a woman running away from someone who was chasing her. As she was looking over her shoulder, her face was wrought with fear. The lady in the dream continued to run until she could no longer see the person behind her. Turning her head forward, she was facing the brightest light she had ever seen.

Hannah asked God, *"What was that you just showed me?"*

With a sigh, God said, *"Hannah, I have been trying to get you and Bubba's attention, and neither of you has taken the time to listen. When you do not listen, your circumstances push you to a breaking point. That woman you just saw was 'you.' You were running from Bubba and danger. That is why you ran towards the bright light. The Light you saw was Me. Hannah, I am the Light. All this time, you have been searching for something, but you did not know what you were looking for. What you have been searching for is Me. You see, when I created you and every human, all my creation was designed to seek after Me. I had to use your situation to get your attention. Did you not know I can use anything to get your attention?*

"You mean you knew this was going to happen to us?" Hannah said.

"Yes, I knew, and I will use it for your good whether you like it or not."

"But this hurts so bad. I want to go home to my family."

"You and Bubba made a choice not to listen to my instructions," God said.

"What instructions?" Hannah asked.

God said, *"Hannah, you and Bubba knew what your marriage vows were. You did not make a promise just between the two of you. More importantly, that promise is a commitment you both made to me. This is where you two went wrong."*

"How did we do that?"

"You left Me out of the picture. When you leave Me out, this is what happens–emptiness and dissatisfaction set in, to name a few. This does not just happen to you and Bubba. This happens to any and everyone who I created. I am the One who gives you strength when you are weak, and that is what you are right now, weak. Just as you were trying to get Bubba's

attention before it was too late, I was trying to get your attention before you got to this point. I am God, and I do not prevent you from making your choices in life. That is your free will."

Hannah shouted, *"Free will! I really need some help here, God. Did you hear me ask my loved ones if they had room for me and my babies to stay with them? Their response was no."*

"Yes, I sure did. You see, Hannah, I knew you would go through this before you were born?" He said.

"Wait just a minute! Then you know I cannot live with Bubba anymore or take his abuse. Huh, did you know that? I want my babies to be taken care of until I can get a home for all of us," she said, twirling around, waving her arms, and stomping her feet like a child.

God said, *"Yes, I sure did. Hannah, I made all the delicate inner parts of your body and knit you together while you were inside your mother's womb. As I said, I knew you before you were born, during your lifetime, and I will know you throughout eternity. I know you, Hannah. Oh, how well do I know you and everybody I created in this world. Your life, every single moment, is recorded in my Book of Life. Hannah, you spent most of your time concerned about Bubba. Your priority should have been Me, but you got it all wrong. You let the enemy fool you into thinking Bubba should be number one."*

ALTHEA P. JONES

"But I did not know you were supposed to be number one in my life." Hannah was very sorrowful after hearing the news that came from God.

"You asked me to do something very important for you, right? I am telling you to do something very important. What I am going to tell you will greatly benefit you and your family and bring me honor," God said.

As she was still dreaming, it seemed as though Hannah had been asleep for a long time. She could hardly wait to hear what it was. Earlier, she was sitting slouched down in her chair like she was barely listening, but now sat straight with her head up and eyes wide opened.

"This is what I want you to do Hannah, I want you to go back home and put your trust in me to work out your situation," God stated.

"No, please, Daddy, do not tell me to go through any more of that abuse," Hannah pleaded. *"After all, you said you saw what happened to me, so why would you tell me to go back there? I do not understand! I do want my children, but I really do not believe that Bubba and I can see eye-to-eye."* It seemed as if Hannah used all her strength to cry out to God about what she thought about her situation.

God could see she was exhausted.

He said, *"I am not asking you to understand. I am telling you to trust me and be patient and allow me time to work out your request. I will not do it without your trust."*

Hannah was ashamed to admit the truth. She whispered, *"To be honest, I do not know what that looks like. I do not believe I ever trusted anyone; I did not even trust Bubba."*

"Well, Hannah, it is great that you ran to the Light. I am here to help you if you surrender. Your weakness is an opportunity for me to help you grow strong now that you are aware of my nearness. Yes, you feel empty because you do not have what it takes to sustain yourself. My power will do that for you." Hannah could hear God's voice sounding like a caring Father.

Hannah started having flashbacks of her life with Bubba. She put her head in her hands and began rubbing her temples as she tried to sort through all that was happening.

"Listen, my child; I will not beg you to trust me. I am always available when you are ready. Once you believe and receive my Son as your Savior, you will have more access to me. I sent my only begotten Son to die for your past, present, and future sins. There will be times you may feel distant, but do not be fooled; that is only a feeling. Please do not get it confused with reality". God continued, *"Hannah, do you know I paid a dear price for you to be free?"*

"I have heard that before but never really had anyone explain it where I could understand."

Hannah had been protected by the One who promised He would never leave her and would always protect her wherever she went. Hannah had no idea how protected she was because she had not understood the importance of believing and receiving Jesus as her Savior. When she was told about Jesus as a child, she was not told that she would face challenging times or that God would be there to see her through those difficult moments in her life.

God went on, *"Now that I have your undivided attention, Hannah, I am going to make this plain enough so you will be able to help yourself, your babies, and Bubba. Hannah, before there was anyone on earth, I knew I was going to be needed by the very humans that I created, but you have to trust me. The only way for you to trust me is to have faith in me, Hannah. You must believe I know what I am doing. I caused Mary to be impregnated supernaturally with my Son, Jesus. He was born knowing his destiny, to be crucified and buried. Crucified means Jesus surrendered his life so you and the world may have life more abundantly here on earth and live eternally in Heaven."*

"Did you say Jesus is your only Son? I have two sons, and I am having a hard time leaving them with Bubba," Hannah said.

"That is because you are not God!" he said.

"You have a point. Go ahead with what you have to say. This is quite interesting," Hannah said.

"I, as a Father, want all of my children to be free. Hannah, you have that opportunity to be free by surrendering and being forgiven. Simply make up your mind who you will serve. Freedom means you will put me first and obey me, before anything and anyone, including Bubba and your children. If you do not do this, you will always be bound to whatever you put in place of me."

"Well, it is up to me to choose, right?" she whispered.

Hannah waited for an answer but nothing. She knew God was telling her the truth. She wanted the peace she was feeling right now to last, so she chose to follow his instructions and receive his Son as her Savior.

CHAPTER 3
MIRACLE AT THE TRAIN STATION

H annah was awakened from her dream by a swishing sound. She yawned and stretched as she felt the warmth of the sun coming through the train station window. As she peered around, she saw the janitor sweeping the floor.

"Good morning," he said. "I did not mean to startle you. If you have any questions about the train schedules or anything else, please ask; I may be able to help you." He was pleasant to her and did not tell her to move or leave the building.

Hannah sat and thought about the long dream she just had. "Boy, that was weird; I just had a conversation with God. It seemed like it lasted forever! She remembered bits and pieces, but it all seemed like a blur. It seemed like God was saying my situation could have been worse than it is. God did not tell me if he was going to do what I asked of him. I do remember believing and receiving his Son as my Lord and Savior. But how am I supposed to know what else to do?"

23

Even though Hannah was sitting in the train station, she did not have enough money to purchase a ticket to go anywhere. She felt so lost and yearned to be with her mom or older sister, who helped raise her. But she was a long way from either of them. She needed someone to talk to, someone who would just listen to her concerns. The thought of leaving her babies behind made Hannah feel distraught and heartbroken. Tears began to flow down her cheeks.

Instead of Hannah walking around the city with her suitcase, she decided to stay in the train station where it seemed to be safe, for the time being. People were coming and going. She could not help but wish she was one of the people getting on the train traveling to see her family.

Hannah overheard a conversation at the ticket counter. A lady had previously purchased a ticket but could not use it because an emergency had occurred. She told the man behind the counter that she wanted a refund. They would not give the lady her money back because they said her ticket was nonrefundable. Both ladies were in need; one had a ticket and could not use it, and Hannah desired a ticket but had no money to purchase one.

The woman turned away from the counter, frustrated. At that very moment, she and Hannah locked eyes. She walked over and extended her hand to Hannah, "Hi, I am Rosie." She explained to Hannah about her situation and where she had planned to travel. Rosie asked Hannah if she could use the ticket.

Almost speechless, Hannah explained she wanted to go to the same city.

Rosie believed Hannah would have better use of the ticket; so, she gave it to Hannah. They went to the counter and worked out the transfer. The results were unbelievable. She thanked Rosie repeatedly. Rosie gave her telephone number to Hannah. "If you ever want to talk, please give me a call. There are no coincidences in the Kingdom of God! So, we must get together, okay?" Rosie said.

"I am grateful to you, Rosie. I can see we would have a lot to talk about."

What was happening seemed so unreal as Hannah stood looking at the ticket with disbelief. Hannah immediately went to the lady's room. She went into one of the stalls and began to cry and pray to God. The words came out jumbled because she was so excited! *"God, I thank you for answering my prayer; you really do listen and answer prayers. Thank you for touching Rosie's heart to bless me with this ticket. What are the chances she was going to the same city I wanted to go to? Thank you so much for taking care of my every need! Please forgive me for not believing that you can do anything! I am getting ready to call my mother to let her know what just happened and to let her know I am on my way to visit,"* Hannah said joyfully.

When Hannah called her mother, there was no answer, so she dialed her eldest sister's number. She was very excited to be able to connect with her. "Hello, Jessica, this is Hannah! Listen, I am at the train station getting ready to come visit. I cannot talk right now because the train is about to board. Please pick me up in the morning at 6:00 a.m. at the same train station you always pick me up at. Okay?" Hannah said.

"Okay, okay, 6:00 a.m. I will be there. Is everything alright?" Jessica said with excitement in her voice.

CHAPTER 4
FEARS AND WORRIES

B ubba and the children awoke the next morning. He noticed Hannah was nowhere to be found in the house.
The children were still in bed. Usually, Hannah would
have awakened early, clothed, and fed them. Bubba could not
figure out what was going on because in all the years they had
been married, she had never strayed from her routine. He went
outside to look around the house, no Hannah. The neighbors
on either side were friendly enough to wave to on occasions.
Bubba decided to take a chance and check with them to see if
they had seen her; they had not. Hannah had never done anything like this before. So, this was a true mystery to him. Bubba
had left the children inside alone, so he hurried back inside.

Bubba went into the girls' room first. They were still in bed
but sat up immediately when they saw him walk in. Sissy and
Lillie looked puzzled when they saw him. Lillie wondered why
her daddy was in their room. They were used to their mom
coming to wake them up.

Sissy said, "Where is Mommy?"

Bubba ran his fingers through his hair and shrugged his shoulders.

Lillie began to cry for her Mommy. Sissy tried to console her with a hug.

"Please, Sissy, get up and put your clothes on and dress your sister for me," Bubba snapped.

Bubba walked down the hall to the boys' room. He instructed Big Bro to get up and get dressed and to help Jacob get his clothes together. Then, Bubba walked back to his bedroom and opened the closet door to see if Hannah's clothes were still there. To his horror, none of her clothes were hanging in the closet–everything was gone. He suddenly felt weak and sick to his stomach. He turned and walked slowly to the dresser. In his mind, he was hoping she had left something. He braced his hand on the dresser to steady his weak body. He slowly opened the drawer where Hannah kept her clothes. To his disappointment, it was empty. In frustration, Bubba took his hand and swept everything off the dresser. He heard the sound of something metal hit the floor. He glanced down to see Hannah's ring rolling across the floor.

Bubba had never imagined this happening to him, of all people. He punched the wall so hard with his fist that he put a hole in it. In his despair, he slid down the wall onto the floor, clutched Hannah's ring, and cried out, "I cannot believe this is happening. Please tell me this is not true."

The loud noise startled the children so much they gasped. They all jumped up and ran down the hall to see what was going on with their daddy. They came to an abrupt halt and stood in the doorway, shocked to see their father sitting on the floor crying. They all knew something was terribly wrong. Big Bro and Jacob stood looking sad because they had never seen him cry before.

Sissy walked over to her daddy and sat down beside him. She patted him on the back and tried to console him, "Daddy, it's going to be okay." It was the spirit of God who gave her the wisdom to say and do what she did. Lillie crawled into her daddy's lap and laid her head on his chest.

"Daddy, are you crying because Mommy is not here? asked Jacob."

"Daddy, where is Mommy?" several of the kids chimed.

With tears streaming down his face, Bubba said, "I don't know, but we're going to find her. The kids wrapped their little arms around each other. Big Bro, Jacob, and Lillie sobbed with him. When Bubba stopped crying, he instructed his children to wipe their faces and finish getting dressed. He looked at Sissy and noticed she had not shed a tear. He wondered what she was thinking.

Bubba washed his face and got himself together. Then he cooked breakfast for everyone. While the kids were eating, he went to make phone calls to family and friends to see if anyone had seen Hannah. No one answered. This frustrated Bubba. He was determined to find her.

After breakfast, Bubba told the children to get in the car so they could take a ride. He drove slowly down the street, looking left and right. He looked carefully at every woman he saw walking and inside cars that passed by–but no Hannah.

Jacob asked, "Are you looking for Mommy?"

Bubba did not answer. He drove to Aunt Ruth's house and parked the car. Bubba said, "Sissy, make sure everyone stays in the car and waits quietly. I'll be right back."

"Okay, Daddy," Sissy said.

When Bubba knocked and went inside. "Ruth, have you seen Hannah?"

Ruth was puzzled that he would ask her about Hannah. She peaked out the window and saw the children in the back seat of the car. She quickly placed her hands over her mouth, "Oh, my goodness, Bubba. Do you think she left you and the children?"

"No! I'm sure that is not what happened. I need you to do me a favor. Please keep the children until I can find out what is going on." Bubba said nervously, pacing the floor.

"Sure, no problem!" Ruth said.

Bubba ran to the car and escorted the children into the house. He knelt down and said softly, "Daddy will be leaving you here with Aunt Ruth, but I will be back to pick you up. Do you understand?" he asked as he looked at each of them. They all nodded their heads and watched as their daddy rushed back to his car.

Bubba got in the car and sat there for a moment, gathering his thoughts. He knew Hannah did not have many friends because she was too busy being a caregiver to her family. So, he wasn't sure where she could be or how he could find her.

What Hannah was doing to Bubba is what he had done to her time and time again. Hannah would be at home with the children night after night while Bubba was out having a good time. Now they were faced with one discouragement after the other. Hannah was not aware that leaving would affect Bubba like this. His emotions were a wreck. He started the car and drove off–going places he thought she might be. He drove up and down the street after street looking to see if he could find his wife. It did not happen. He had no clue where she could be. He decided he needed to go to a quiet place where he could think–so he went home.

Bubba opened the door, hoping to hear Hannah's voice calling out to him. But he was greeted with silence. He sat in his chair and put his head in his hands. This situation has stretched him to the limit. The thought of losing his family was very painful for him. Bubba had a good idea why Hannah decided to leave. He knew he needed to become a better husband to Hannah and a better father to the children if he wanted to keep his family together. He stood up and began pacing back and forth and began to talk out loud.

"I heard her say she was tired, but I did not know she was that tired—tired enough to leave her babies and me. If I want her to return, I know I need to get my act together. But I work hard to make sure my family has a roof over their heads and food and clothes. What more does she want from me? If I give any more, I will not have a life of my own."

Bubba was thinking about his life with Hannah. Usually, when he got off work, he would go hang out with his buddies and drink–drowning his pain and frustration. It was seldom he was sober around his family. He thought Hannah was okay with their life but realized that her actions in the past twenty-four hours showed him she was not happy at all. He walked to the kitchen and opened the refrigerator. There was one beer inside–it looked so tempting he just wanted to reach inside and get the beer to soothe his nerves.

"No, no, this is what got me here in the first place!" he shouted angrily. He closed the refrigerator door and paused with his hand still on the handle. He pulled the door open again and picked up the beer. Just as he was opening the bottle, the phone rang. He put the beer on the counter and went to the living room, knocking over a chair while almost falling trying to

answer the phone before it stopped ringing. He prayed it was Hannah calling.

"Hello, Hannah! Hannah, is this you?" Bubba said frantically. No one was there. Bubba could hear the dial tone buzzing in his ear. Apparently, the person had hung up. He stood there holding the phone to his chest. By now, Bubba was so stressed he left the beer on the counter and went to lie down on the sofa. After a few minutes, he drifted off to sleep.

Chapter 5
Tough Decisions

I n his dream, he heard his name being called, "Bubba! Bubba!" The voice that was calling him was not familiar. He heard the voice a third time.

"Bubba!" the voice was even more stern.

"Huh? I mean, yes! Who is calling my name?" Confused, Bubba repeated, "Who is calling my name?"

"I Am!" the Voice said.

"Well, what kind of name is that?" Bubba said to the voice.

"I Am the One you need to help you with your difficult situations," said the voice.

Bubba asked, "Really, how do you know about my situation?"

"You see, you cannot hide or keep secrets because I know every thought before you think it and every move you make before you make it. I even know what you are going to do after you awake from this dream. I am going to give you some wise

35

instructions, and I command you to follow them! Do you understand?" I Am was talking to Bubba in a very authoritative tone.

Bubba's facial expression was one his children would make when they were in trouble. With a childish look like his son Jacob had made, he answered, "Yes, I understand."

Looking for I Am was troubling for Bubba; he could only hear his voice. I Am's voice was not boisterous; he talked in a tone and speed where Bubba could clearly hear and understand.

"Bubba, you have been so busy ignoring me you were destined to have difficulties. You are at the crossroad where you will have to make a choice which road you will travel, yours or mine. I am glad you did not drink that beer. Now you are sober enough for me to talk to you with an open heart and a clear mind. I am a jealous God, and you have put everyone before me. I tried to get your attention way before now, but you ignored me. Now here we are." This was all new to Bubba, so he continued to listen. I Am continued. *"Leaving your parent's home at an early age has caused your blessings to be cut short."*

"How did I do that?" Bubba asked.

I Am explained to Bubba how he had given a commandment to his children long ago. *"Children, obey your father and mother, for this is right. Bubba, how can you obey your father and mother if you were not home? Unfortunately, you took a woman as your bride and did not know how to love her.*

Hannah is my daughter, and you have mistreated the precious gift I gave you. Because you did not learn how to love yourself, you could not love Hannah. Bubba, there is a way for you to get on the right track, but only if you choose to do so."

"What do I have to do? Hannah had already asked if I would be home more than being with my friends. When she asked, I thought she did not want me to have any more fun," Bubba said.

"Bubba, the time has passed for you to have fun with your friends. You are a man now. Being responsible and having fun with your family is what you should be doing. If you focus on the obstacle, which you call fun, or search for another way around what I told you, you will find yourself right back in the same situation or even worse. As I said earlier, either do what I have commanded you or else your life will continue to go down a destructive path."

The Lord paused a while longer to make sure he had Bubba's undivided attention. I Am was giving him time to begin confessing his sins. Bubba thought I Am had left because he was silent. "Are you still there?" Bubba asked.

"Certainly, I would never leave you," he said. *"But this is a warning to you, surrender and be forgiven, Bubba!"*

Bubba, seeming disappointed, said, "I am listening to your instructions because I really want to get my life together."

"Do you want to get your life together because you feel lost without Hannah? Or do you want to because it is the right thing to do? I suggest including me in your life, Bubba! You cannot get yourself together by yourself. You need my help! Up to this point, you have been a type of god over your life. If you want to get your life together, right now is a great time to start. Are you thankful for anything? As you listen and obey me, there are many benefits for you. The first is obvious, it will keep the lines of communication open with me, and it will continue to give you the strength to turn your issues into opportunities. You will have a constant Guide throughout each day. I had planned your days before you were formed in your mother's womb. These are important pieces you need to get through this battle you are in. I'm not saying you will not have trouble in your life. But you will have help getting through your trials, if this is what you want," I Am said.

"I have not enjoyed being drunk or disrespecting Hannah and the children. It appears life has sucked me up, and I thought I had nowhere to turn. Drinking was the only thing I could drown my sorrows in. Hannah imagined I was having fun, but it was not that at all. Most of the time, I would laugh to keep from crying. There were times I decided to sit in the car and cry before going inside the house."

Bubba slowly began to kneel while speaking. He knew this showed respect and honor. He continued, "God, as I stated earlier, I do want to change. I want to start by saying I am sorry for not loving you first, myself, and your daughter, Hannah, properly. I know all good things, including my possessions, my health, wealth, abilities, family, and friends, and even my time are gifts from you. I do not deserve any of it; instead, I have acted as if I am privileged. I know I should show you that I am grateful." Bubba sounded more sorrowful than ever before.

I Am was appreciative that Bubba was pouring out his heart to him, but there were more important truths he had to share with him.

"Bubba, there comes a time in a man's life when he needs to make concrete decisions. You clearly see the path you have traveled and have a good idea where you are headed if you do not obey. No one can make this decision for you. As much as you say you want to be with Hannah, she cannot make the decision for you. The most important choice you must make in life is who you will serve!"

Bubba said, "What you are telling me is really confusing right now!"

I Am proceeded, *"Okay, I will say this in a simplistic way because I do not want you to be confused. You have a house, correct? The roof and outer walls protect the inner wall, and the inner walls protect you, your family, and your personal belongings. Do you understand so far?"*

"I get it now," Bubba said.

I Am saw that Bubba was very engaged, so he continued. *"You can see and feel your flesh or body, which is also your temple. It is the house for my Spirit, the Holy Spirit, that you or anyone who receives my Son, Jesus, will live. Bubba, I already know the question you want to ask. How can you receive my Son? Great question! This is how you do so. You must begin believing in your heart that Jesus died on the cross for your sins and was buried and resurrected. The only reason he died is because you and every human needed a Savior. Otherwise, everyone would go to hell. Once you believe, you must surrender and ask for forgiveness. Then, confess that you are a sinner and receive my Son."*

"When you pray, say, 'Dear God, please forgive me of my sins. The sins I know I have committed and those I am not aware of. I know I have not obeyed your commands, and I am sorry. Today I have learned so much about you. I believe Jesus died for my sins. I believe he is coming back to receive me. I make a conscious decision to receive Jesus as my Lord and Savior. Thank you for loving me and leading me into eternal life. In the Precious and Mighty Name of Jesus, I pray. Amen.'"

"Bubba, I encourage you to say the prayer, but I cannot make you. When and if you decide, you will secure the home for your spirit that will be in heaven eternally. This is the only way your house can be purified. If you decide not to obey me, your spirit will automatically go to hell. I already know you have gone through life without thinking about anything I am

saying. I am the only One who knows when you will take your last breath. Now you have heard my instructions, do you think you are ready, right here and now? You get to decide who you are going to live for—Me or the Devil! I say again, I cannot and will not make the decision for you!

"Come on!" Bubba said in discouragement. "You want an answer right now? Don't I get time to think about this before making a decision? You did tell me I am the only one who could decide."

I Am reminded Bubba that He is the only One who is able to help him out of the mess he had gotten himself in.

"Making a choice right now is insane!" he said.

"You are weak and weary; I come to give you rest. I am drawn to you when you are weak because this is when my power is made strong within you. Bubba, you need to quiet your heart and mind so you can hear me speak. Right now, you are all worked up over a command I have given you. I gave this command at the beginning of time. There is no need for you to get frustrated. Rest in me, my child. Coming to me will require a great effort on your part, but it is not impossible," I Am said.

Still looking puzzled, Bubba said, "You mean I have to work, too?"

"Bubba, you are already working and not getting the best results. You are working harder without me. Redirect your

41

focus towards me and not on your troubles. I will help you," I Am said, with assurance.

Still dreaming, Bubba was torn between his comfortable lifestyle and the command given by God. Bubba should not have had to think long about his decision. I Am made it perfectly clear as to what he needed to do and how to go about making his decision. The Devil's job is to steal, kill, and destroy him if he decided not to follow I Am's instructions. Bubba began to curl up into a fetal position and shake as he struggled to figure out what to do. Satan began flashing seductive women in his mind at the same time I Am was speaking to him. A smile came across Bubba's face. He was caught in a trap.

"Bubba, I am waiting on you to choose," said I Am.

The Devil was trying to awake him before he answered the important question I Am had asked. Bubba kicked his legs and rolled side-to-side as if he were trying to get away from someone holding him. He cried out, *"Please forgive me. I am sorry."* Bubba woke up. He rubbed his eyes and looked around. He thought he was in a strange place but saw that he was in his own home. "What just happened? Where was I? I must have been dreaming," Bubba said.

He began to think about the dream he had. "Did I just meet God who said his name was I Am? That was crazy! Why would he say his name is I Am instead of God?" As he got off the floor, he walked from room to room, remembering portions of what I Am had said. He began to repeat it out loud:

"Here and now, I want you to decide who you are going to live for, Me, yourself, or the Devil. Rest in me, my child. You are already working and not getting the best results. Redirect your focus on Me. I will help you! You must begin believing in your heart Jesus died on the cross for your sins and that he was buried and resurrected. The only reason he died is because you and every human needed a Savior. Bubba, I am waiting on you to choose."

Subsequently, Bubba found that putting his fun and drinking before Hannah and his family was not honoring God. Hannah and the children should have been his first responsibility, but he neglected his head of household status. Hiding behind his alcohol caused him to not see life the way it really was. As God talked with Bubba and gave him a warning to surrender and be forgiven, Bubba thought it would be too difficult to give up alcohol and hanging out with his friends on his own. But God told him that He would help him through this change and would walk beside him and never leave him. He told Bubba he was not going to guarantee that Hannah would return even if he made the changes God was requesting. Bubba said he understood.

God reminded Bubba it would be hard to have a relationship with Him when he was trying to live on his own strength. The enemy did not want Bubba to do as God had instructed him to. However, Bubba made the right decision at the right time by receiving Jesus as his Lord

and Savior. Then, he learned to put his family first. Although it was hard, Bubba knew he had what it takes to live a life that is pleasing to God.

CHAPTER 6
LIFE WITHOUT HANNAH

H annah was still visiting her sister Jessica. She went to a quiet place in the house to use the phone to call Bubba.

Suddenly, Bubba's phone rang in the living room. Bubba was in the bathroom. As he headed in that direction, he jumped over the coffee table and grabbed the phone before it stopped ringing. To his surprise, it was Hannah. She was crying uncontrollably as she spoke the painful words, "I am through trying to please you and take care of the children alone. I will not be..." Hannah could hardly finish her sentence as she was crying so hard. "Bubba, I will...I will..." It was extremely hard for her to get the words out.

"Slow down, Hannah. I cannot understand a word you are saying," Bubba said. He was listening closely, hoping she would tell him where she was so he could go get her.

"I will not be coming back home."

"Please, please do not do this to me!" Bubba begged. "There is no way I can take care of these children without you, Hannah," he said frantically.

"Bubba, I tried to tell you for years how tired I was with you not helping me. I will not do it anymore!"

Bubba had not heard her sound so serious before, so he pleaded once again. Hannah told him she felt she was not loved or wanted by him. He exclaimed, "Hannah, I promise I will do better! Listen, I need to see you so I can tell you about this dream I had!"

Hannah was shocked and speechless that Bubba mentioned having a dream because she too had a dream and had an important decision to make. It took a lot out of Hannah to decide to leave. Going back to receive the same treatment is not what she was willing to do.

As she was about to hang up, she heard Bubba shouting, "Hannah! Hannah! Hannah, please do not..."

Bubba heard the dial tone buzzing in his ear. He looked at the phone and dropped it. He was very exhausted from his dream and from receiving the bad news from Hannah. He knew he was in a hard place in his life. He remembered I Am telling him that he would help him if Bubba was willing to work on his relationship with Hanna. I AM also told him that He would be there for him. Bubba knew that I Am did not push himself onto anyone and allows everyone free will to make their own choices. Bubba knew he had been warned, so he had to make a decision soon, and he wanted to make the best decision for him and his family.

It was getting dark, and the children had been at Ruth's house all day. Bubba was really hurting emotionally, but he knew he needed to go pick the children up. He pulled himself together and called Ruth to let her know he would be on his way. When he walked in the door, the children ran up to him as if he had been gone for days. They really did miss him, and they missed their Mommy too.

"Have you heard from Hannah?" Ruth asked.

Bubba did not want to discuss the situation in front of the children. "Let me get the children in the car because it is getting late. I will talk to you later, okay?"

Ruth said, "No problem. Take your time. I cannot imagine how you must feel."

On the way home, the children were quiet until Sissy said, "Did you talk to Mommy yet?"

Bubba stumbled over his words because he did not want to lie, nor did he want her to worry.

"Yes, and she is fine. Mommy told me to tell each of you she loves you and will see you soon."

Lillie said, "Tonight?" She had leaned forward, hoping her daddy would say, *"Sure."*

But instead, Bubba said, "Soon."

Sissy could sense things were not right with her Daddy and Mommy. Big Bro and Jacob sat in silence.

Two weeks had passed, and Hannah had not returned home. Bubba and the children made it through the best they could. Before Hannah left home, Bubba did not come home before the children went to bed. Now, he is very concerned about the children since he is the only one taking care of them and seeing about their needs. Life had become very difficult for him, but day after day, somehow, he made it through. Bubba knew he could not continue the way it was, so he began to seek help.

Since Sissy was the oldest, she helped out around the house. She made sure her siblings got their baths before going to bed, put their clothes out for the next day, and prepared simple meals for everyone. Big Bro was beginning to be rebellious towards her and not listening to what she said. Sissy would instruct Big Bro to do his chores, but he would be late starting or not completing them at all. In order for her to get him to be in unity, she would bribe him with something he really wanted to have, like extra snacks.

Mama Hannah taught Sissy how to operate the washer and dryer, fold the clothes and put them away. Laundry was always one of the biggest chores, even when Mama Hannah was home. Because there were so many people in their family, it took two people to get the laundry done. Now is the time for Big Bro to learn what she knew so he could help out. "Big Bro, I need you to help me with laundry today."

"I do not know how to do laundry, and you know that!" Big Bro said.

"Yes, I know that. There was a time I did not know how to do laundry either! I will show you just like Mama Hannah showed me. Please come get the clothes out of the dryer and put them on the bed. We will separate them into two piles, boys' clothes, and girls' clothes. We will start with your pile over here—let's place yours and Jacob's stuff near the head of the bed, and I'll put Lillie and my clothes at the foot of the bed. See how easy that was, Big Bro? Now, you try it."

"Okay." Big Bro followed Sissy's instruction until all the clothes were in their proper pile. "Am I done?"

"No, you are not! We need to fold them and put them away. Let me show you how to fold."

"But I do not want to learn how to do this!"

"Yes, you do! You just do not know it yet."

Sissy could see Big Bro was getting frustrated, so she told him she would give him some ice cream when they finished. He smiled and agreed to help fold the clothes. He watched Sissy fold the shirts and soon caught on. "Now, when you finish, put your things away, and then tell Jacob to put his stuff away. I will help Lillie with hers."

Sissy left Big Bro and went to put another load of clothes she had washed into the dryer. When she returned, she was surprised to see Big Bro had done a great job! She looked at the piles of folded clothes, then looked at him and smiled. "Big Bro, you're kidding me."

"What do you mean?" He did not understand what Sissy was saying. When he saw her big smile, he smiled too.

"I thought you said you did not know how to do laundry. You did an outstanding job! Come here." Sissy gave him a big hug. The hug made Big Bro feel good about his accomplishments.

CHAPTER 7
THE GIFT OF GIVING

◆

C lose friends and relatives heard that Hannah had left home and knew Bubba could not take care of his four young children on his own. The ladies all got together and had a meeting about who was going to do what and when. They organized themselves to become caregivers to Bubba and the children. After several months since the caregivers began, life had turned around considerably for Bubba and the children.

One lady, Victoria, who was not a relative, was not just helping just to help; she had an agenda. She seemed to have one eye overlooking the well-being of the children, and the other eye was on Bubba. While Bubba was at work, the women had conversations about him. Some of the ladies were talking about how everything seemed to be working out better for the family since they had been helping Bubba. They had also noticed how Victoria seemed to put in extra time at the house caring for Bubba and the kids.

It was quite apparent that Bubba had an eye for Victoria. He always thought he was a lady's man. Some days, she would come earlier than usual so she and Bubba could have coffee together before he left for work. Other days she would stay late, so she could prepare a special dinner for him and the children. This was happening more and more.

After about a year, Bubba told the other ladies he had found permanent help and would no longer need them. They were not surprised because they had noticed Bubba and Victoria spending more and more time together. As a matter of fact, they encouraged the relationship since it did not look like Hannah was going to return, and they knew Victoria was single with no children.

CHAPTER 8
FIRST GENERATION BLENDED FAMILY

❧

Victoria and Bubba's relationship grew closer. He invited her to come live with him and the children. She had already established a connection with them, so the transition was easy. Life seemed to have become more stable. Victoria was there day after day just like Hannah was. The children were happy that their father was happy. He also seemed to be at home more since Victoria was there. Bubba had become comfortable with how things were going, but he still missed Hannah. There were times when they all would be joking around, but their father would be staring off as if he were in another world.

The days and months seemed to have flown by. Little by little, Bubba became more comfortable with his new arrangement. He started slipping back into his old ways of drinking and staying out late like he did when Hannah was home. This caused him and Victoria to start drifting apart. At the beginning of their relationship, Bubba kept his drinking under control, but now it was totally different.

Victoria assumed Bubba was still hurting because of the burden of taking care of his children without Hannah being there to help. She thought this probably drove him back to drinking. Victoria sat on the sofa thinking, "*Before meeting Bubba, I was as free as a bird! No husband and no children! The only person I had to care of was me. Now, here I am, living in a home with a man who has four children, and he is an alcoholic. I'm living an adulterous lifestyle. What the heck was thinking?*" The thought of all that did not sit well with her.

Victoria had always wanted to be married. She envisioned her, Bubba, and the children being a close-knit family. That is why she gave her all to be their caregiver. Whatever she needed to do to get Bubba back on track, she was willing to give it a try. She thought about the rumors she had heard, how he had treated his wife and never had time for his family. But she thought things would be different for her and Bubba.

Bubba came home, stumbling as he walked in. He heard Victoria humming in the kitchen. She was washing the dinner dishes and putting everything away. He went towards her and tried to give her a kiss. She smelled alcohol on him and pulled away. Bubba got upset and grabbed her arms, trying to force her to give him a kiss. Victoria pushed him so hard he fell against the wall. This only made Bubba angry. "What the hell are you doing?"

"Bubba, please do not start being rude to me! I have done nothing but be nice to you! Go into the room and get some sleep. There is no reason to get violent!" Bubba started coming towards her. She picked up a knife out of the dishrack to protect herself.

Bubba stopped abruptly and looked at Victoria, confused. "You trying to hurt me?"

The yelling woke Lillie up. Lillie climbed out of bed and peaked around the corner of the kitchen to see what was going on. She saw a knife in Victoria's hand. She was scared that her father was in danger. She hurried and ran to get back into bed, quickly throwing the covers over her head. Lillie did not want to think about waking up the next morning and seeing her father or Victoria hurt. So, she covered her ears until she drifted off to sleep.

Bubba and Victoria continued to argue. Victoria said, "No, I do not want to hurt you, Bubba." She had never been in a situation like this before, so she did not know what to expect. He was not the Bubba she knew once he was drunk. "Bubba, I don't want to argue with you anymore. Let's just go to bed."

The next morning Lillie peaked out her bedroom door to see if everything was okay. Her daddy was asleep in bed, and Victoria was preparing breakfast. Although she was saddened by what she saw last night, things seemed back to normal now. So, she got dressed and sat at the kitchen table. Her brothers and sisters soon joined her. As usual, a bowl of oatmeal was waiting for her and her siblings so they could eat before going to school. "Where's my daddy?" Lillie asked.

"Eat your food, and do not worry about your daddy!" Victoria snapped.

All of the kids looked shocked at Mama Victoria's comment. Lillie looked hurt but did not say anything. She did not understand why Mama Victoria seemed so angry.

When they finished their breakfast, the four siblings walked to school together. They did not laugh or joke like they usually did. They walked with their heads down, saddened by all the chaos in their home. Their home had become an environment filled with constant anger. Victoria had changed. She seemed angry all the time, probably because Daddy Bubba was hardly ever home anymore. It was a good thing they were in school, so they could get away from the chaos for a few hours. At least the teachers and other adults at school were nice to them. And they enjoyed getting to be with their friends.

At the end of the school day, it was time to do it all over again. Sissy would wait for each of them at their designated meeting spot. Once they were all together, they would walk home. Sissy felt it was her duty to make sure the rest of the siblings got home safely from school and felt comforted since Mama Hannah was no longer with them.

As soon as they got in the door, Sissy told her siblings to put their school stuff away. Big Bro hit Sissy. "I'm tired of you always trying to tell me what to do."

"Why did you hit me, Big Bro? I'm just trying to help. I'm going to tell Mama Victoria."

Big Bro, "I don't care."

Mama Victoria rushed into the living room. "What's going on?" No one said a word. "Big Bro, I'm concerned about your behavior. You seem to always be mad. I'm disappointed that you keep fighting with your brothers and sisters."

Big Bro asked, "Why are you so concerned about me? You are not my real mother."

"Big Bro, just go to your room, please. I'm not going to put up with all of this talking back. I'll talk to your daddy about this when he gets home."

Mama Victoria genuinely cared for all the children. However, she was concerned that Bubba did not spend enough time with his kids. Sometimes Bubba's actions seemed as though he did not want a family. Was that the reason he stayed gone so much? When Bubba was not too drunk, he would sometimes come home before the children went to bed. He would often play with them like father and children are supposed to. They all seemed to really enjoy these good times, which brought a lot of laughter in the home. However, he was not home most of the time. Maybe that's why Big Bro was acting out so much because he missed spending time with his daddy. Sometimes Mama Victoria would sit and watch the kids play and have fun, but she seldom joined in. She wanted to, but for some reason, she never did.

CHAPTER 9
THE SECOND BLENDED FAMILY

Mama Hannah knew that trying to blend her two families together would cause a lot of stress since the children were not aware they had two sets of parents. She figured they would need to say Mama and Daddy in front of all the parents' given names to help keep the confusion down. So, they would continue to call her "Mama Hannah, and her new husband can be called Daddy Matthews. Of course, they will still call their father Daddy Bubba, and continue to call Victoria, Mama Victoria.

Periodically, Mama Hannah went to visit the children. Most of the time, their father was not home. During one of Mama Hannah's visits, Sissy asked, "Since you are our real mother, Mama Hannah, why can't you stay with us?"

Hannah could not answer Sissy's question. In her heart, she always felt like Mama Victoria was always listening to their conversations. So, she didn't want to say anything to upset her or anything that would cause her to tell Bubba something that would make him upset with her or the kids. "Sissy, I can't stay with you, but I will be coming back to visit," said Mama Hannah.

Sissy said, "Well, I want to go with you."

"Maybe next time," Mama Hannah said joyfully. "Your dad will not let you go with me this time."

Sissy watched Mama Hannah as she prepared to leave. "Mama Hannah, please, can I go with you?"

"I promise I will be back to see you, Sissy. And not only will I come back to see you, but I will bring you a very special gift."

Sissy's eyes got big, and she hugged Mama Hannah tight and then looked up at her with a big smile. The other children stood beside Sissy, waiting to give Hannah a hug. As Mama Hannah approached the door, they each gave her a big hug. Mama Hannah smiled and walked down the steps to her car. When she reached the car, she glanced back at the children. She backed out of the driveway, waved goodbye, and headed home.

Mama Victoria gathered the children and said, "I hope you enjoyed your visit with Mama Hannah. But it is time to get ready for bed."

"Alright," Big Bro said and looked at Jacob. "Come on."

Lillie and Sissy headed down the hall to their bedroom. They slept in the same room, same bed. Sissy told Lillie she was going to live with Mama Hannah. It was too confusing to Lillie.

She didn't want her big sister to leave her, so she started to cry. Sissy told her not to cry and not to worry because she was not going to be leaving any time soon. Lillie hugged her big sister, and soon they fell asleep.

When Daddy Bubba came home from work that night, Mama Victoria told him Hannah came to visit. Daddy Bubba was not pleased about the news. As a matter of fact, he became furious about it and hit the wall with his fist. Mama Victoria did not understand why he would not let Hannah come to see her own children. She began to wonder, *"What could she have done that was so bad she was not allowed to visit her own children? Was he still angry about her leaving the children with him? Could he have wanted her to stay, and she refused?"* Victoria tried to calm him down, but this only made him angrier. "What's wrong, Bubba?"

Bubba rolled his eyes at her but did not say anything. When Victoria asked again what was wrong, Bubba started yelling at her about letting Mama Hannah in the house when he was not home. Victoria thought it was best to let him vent until he got tired and went to bed.

The next morning Sissy asked Mama Victoria why she and her dad were arguing. Mama Victoria told Sissy that Daddy Bubba was angry because she told him about Mama Hannah coming to visit. This made Sissy very sad because she didn't understand why her dad did not want her mother to visit them.

After breakfast, she and her siblings got ready to leave for school. As they were walking, Sissy told Lillie, "You better not say anything about our secret I mentioned to you last night." Lillie looked confused. She did not understand what a secret was because no one had ever explained it to her. Sissy reminded her not to say anything to anyone.

"Okay! I will not say anything!" Lillie said and threw her hands up in frustration.

After school, the children went straight home. They were surprised to see their Daddy was there. They were extremely excited because it was the first time he had gotten home before them, and he was not drunk. Daddy walked over to Sissy and looked her straight in the eyes, and said, "Sissy, I do not want you to ask if you can go with your Mama Hannah ever again! Do you understand me?" he said sternly.

Sissy began to tremble, "Yes." She really wanted to know why she could not go live with her mother. All Sissy wanted was something different than what she had been given so far as a child. She was searching for what all children need when they enter into this world, love and affection. She felt what she was giving out to her siblings should have been given back to her, from someone important, like her Mama Hannah and Daddy.

Days turned into months and then into years since Sissy had said anything else about living with her Mama Hannah. When her mother was allowed to visit, Sissy stayed her distance and did not go ask to stay with Hannah because she did not want to be rejected again or to make her daddy upset with her. It bothered Sissy that she could not live with her mother. Although she did not ask if she could live with Mama Hannah, it did not stop her from thinking about it every single day.

After many years had passed, Mama Hannah had divorced Bubba and married a man named Matthew. They had three children. She was focused on trying to build her new home with her new husband. During this time, Hannah had not seen or talked to her children that she had with Bubba, nor communicated with him. She was not sure how she could tell her old family about her new family or the new family about her old family. So, for years, none of Hannah's children knew they had other siblings living just a few miles away.

One day Sissy overheard Mama Victoria's phone conversation. They were talking about Hannah having a new family. This shocked Sissy because she had not heard anything about her mother having another family. *"Is that why she won't let me come live with her?"* This weighed heavily on Sissy's heart.

Since Mama Hannah got married again, her visits became fewer. When she did visit, Sissy was not clinging to her as she had before. When she arrived, Sissy could see that Mama Hannah kept her promise. In her hands were a doll and some clothes. The other children only received clothes. Mama Hannah noticed that Sissy was acting stand-offish. Sissie's siblings usually followed what she did, and that day was no different. The kids were usually so excited and happy when she came to visit. Their behavior was confusing to her. Mama Hannah looked at Sissy's sad face. She knelt to hold the doll with one hand, and the other she placed on Sissy's back. "Do you like the surprise I bought for you?"

Sissy nodded her head, "Yes."

Mama Hannah could sense that something was wrong. She kissed Sissy and hugged her tight. "Sissy, you do know you can talk to me about how you feel, right?"

Sissy nodded her head yes. Since Sissy was the oldest, Mama Hannah was more concerned about her. She knew Sissy was having a hard time adjusting to Mama Hannah being in and out of her life. During her visits, Mama Hannah talked and played with her other children, too. She loved and missed them as much as she did Sissy. Big Bro, Jacob, and Lillie were not as concerned about going to live with her as Sissy was. As usual, when Mama Hannah got ready to leave, she gave each of the children a big kiss and hug and told them she loved them and that she would see them very soon. It was getting increasingly difficult for Mama Hannah to come and go, with Sissy feeling and acting the way she was.

When Daddy Bubba arrived home, he saw that Mama Hannah had visited. The new clothes were lying across the chair, and Sissy was holding the doll she was given. Even though Daddy Bubba saw the evidence, he yelled, "Did she come over here again?"

Mama Victoria yelled back, "Why would you ask that question? If you look around, you can see that she did! I do not understand why you cannot let the kids go visit her!"

For years Sissy had been waiting for a perfect time to say what she had always wanted to say. "I want to go live with her anyway. She is my mother!" Sissy stomped her foot.

This inspired Lillie to speak up, "I want to go with my Sissy." Lillie knew she did not want to be left behind.

Daddy Bubba looked at both of them as he slumped into the chair at the kitchen table. He placed his head in his hands. His soft black wavy hair fell over his hands. It was obvious he was sad and confused. At that very moment, it seemed like the weight of the world was on his shoulders. It was obvious the whole situation put him in a tailspin. After several minutes, Daddy Bubba raised his head; his eyes were red. He shook his head as if trying to sort through what the kids had asked. It was obvious he had been crying, but he did not let any of them see the tears. As a man, he wanted to always appear strong and in control.

Mama Victoria glanced at all of them. She was disappointed and speechless that she had come into a family like this—what a mess.

Daddy Bubba stood up; he brushed his hair away from his face and took a deep breath. "Alright, let me see if the two of you can go stay with *her.*" It was obvious it hurt him to say the words, "Your *Mother.*"

This seemed like an awkward moment. Everyone was quiet and began looking around the room at each other. No one expected Daddy Bubba to give in so easily. They watched as he picked up the phone to call Mama Hannah.

He pulled a piece of folded paper out of his pocket with Hannah's number written on it. All eyes were on him, so he walked down the hallway with the phone as he was dialing. Her phone began to ring. Someone answered the phone. He lowered his voice, "Hello, may I speak to Hannah?" Bubba had not talked to Hannah for a long time, he did not recognize her voice, and she did not recognize his.

"This is Hannah."

"This is Bubba. I am calling to make sure it is okay for Sissy and Lillie to come live with you. They asked me if they could go, and I told them I would check."

"Yes, Bubba, I have made arrangements for them to come. Let's figure out a date that I can come by and get Sissy and Lillie. Unfortunately, I have not been able to work out the accommodations for the boys yet."

Bubba sighed, "Okay, that is all I called for." He put the phone on the hook and went into his room. *"That's it,"* Bubba thought. *"Sissy and Lillie will be going to live with Hannah."* He placed his hand on his heart; this was almost unbearable.

Even though he knew this day would come, he did not want his girls to leave; he did not want his family separated.

The last visit Hannah had with the children at Bubba's house caused her a lot of anguish. She decided she needed to talk to her husband, Matthew. Hannah was hoping the conversation would be quick and painless. When she and Matthew had gotten together, they discussed the possibility of Hannah's children coming to live with them. But Bubba did not want Hannah to have contact with the children since they were not together. Matthew did not want the children to live with him and Hannah because he felt it was Bubba's responsibility to take care of his own children. The two men's jealousy was causing problems for Hannah. She was put in an awkward position because the men were not thinking about what was best for her children. They were only thinking about their own selfish feelings of jealousy. Hannah had to put her desire to have her children living with her on hold.

Hannah decided to confront Matthew. She wanted him to understand her dilemma. "You have no idea what it feels like for me to keep going over there to visit my children that I birthed into the world and not be able to bring them home with me," she said as she pounded her hand against her chest. "Matthew, I need you to hear me with your heart! When we first met, we agreed that the children would come to live with us, did we not? You said, 'Yes, to having a blended family and that we would work together. The time is now. Whatever you need to do to fix this, you better hurry up and do it. I am not going to wait much longer! I know we do not have a big house, but we can arrange this one to work for all of us," she cried out. She took a couple of deep breaths to reel herself back into her peaceful state of mind.

Matthew was lost for words. He stared at Hannah but did not respond to her. He had never seen that side of Hannah.

Hannah took a step back and began looking around the house. Her eyes lit up as she visualized how the arrangement could work. She folded her arms across her chest, content that she had solved the problem.

Hannah felt she had been pushed against the wall too many times regarding her children. She was not the same person when she walked out on Bubba and the kids. Hannah had matured into a woman who knew what she wanted, and she was not going to accept anything less. She had become strong, responsible, and eager to make the best of her life. Her life was stable, and she was employed. Hannah had not forgotten the courage it took to get her to this point. She was willing to take another big leap of faith on behalf of her children so they could come live with her. There comes a time when a mother must do what her gut feeling tells her. Hannah knew she had to start making plans to move her children. Although Matthew said "yes" with his mouth, he did not help like she had hoped he would. She accepted that she might have to do this alone.

CHAPTER 10
ANTICIPATION

annah knew that Sissy was yearning for her attention, and she was more than ready to give it. A mother's bonding is very different from that of a father's bonding. Neither Bubba nor Matthew had any idea of what Hannah was going through physically, mentally, or spiritually living without her babies. However, they were great providers but lacked in their ability to show affection and empathy. Hannah was not going to let how they felt towards each other stop her from doing the right thing for her children. She was thankful Bubba had Victoria in his life. She noticed how she had developed a loving, caring relationship with children she had not given birth to. Because of this, Hannah respected Victoria and was able to easily be friendly towards her.

When Matthew and Hannah married, they bought a home with three bedrooms. There was a twin bed and dresser in the room for Mama Hannah's daughter, Jewel. It was time for Mama Hannah to show how determined she was in getting her children. She was good about staying on task to make things happen. The girls' room needed another bunk bed and another dresser, so she went out and bought them. When the furniture was delivered, Daddy Matthew became grumpy because he had to help. This annoyed Hannah. As the head of the family, he was responsible for setting the tone for the family. Instead, he made it uncomfortable at times. Hannah could not help but think back to the time when her and Bubba were living together in their home. He also could make life unbearable.

Mama Hannah always knew the time would come to bring up the subject of a blended family. Mama Hannah decided to go ahead and face her fears. She knew the topic may be difficult, but she welcomed it because she knew it was time. She gathered her husband, Daddy Matthew, along with their children, Jewel, Oscar, and Sam, and told them to have a seat in their family room.

"I want to discuss with you what is about to happen in our home," she said.

The family structure in their home was how God designed it to be, a husband as head of the household, a wife, and children.

Mama Hannah led the conversation with Jewel sitting very close to her and her brothers sitting on the floor looking up at their mother.

Mama Hannah said, "You all have been taught about loving each other and loving others, right?"

The children could see the look on her face was quite serious. They nodded their heads in agreement and were eager to hear what more she had to say. She continued, "I think you have done a great job respecting and loving one another as we have taught you. We want you to know how proud we are for doing so. With that said, I have some very exciting, as well as important news to tell you."

Their eyes widened, and each of them sat up and listened closely. I have wanted to tell you this before now, but the time was not right. We believe the time is right now."

Oscar chimed in, "Okay, please tell us, we can't wait to hear what you're going to say."

"Way back before your dad and I were married, I had another family. In that family are two more brothers and two more sisters. I want you to meet them very soon." Hannah's eyes looked at Matthew and each of her children when she spoke. This was her first time saying these words aloud, even though she had wanted to many times before. The children did not say anything; they just stared at Mama. She felt very uncomfortable because the children sat silent, not saying a word. She asked, "Did you hear what I just said?"

The children looked shocked. They had never heard such a thing, so they did not know how to react. They just sat motionless, staring at their mother.

"I told you we should have waited," Daddy Matthew said, not making things any better.

Mama Hannah looked at her children, surprised by their silence, but she was not going to let this change the fact they needed to meet their other brothers and sisters. Mama Hannah came up with an idea, "I know everyone loves ice cream, so why don't we have an ice cream party and invite them to join us?"

The children snapped out of their speechless moment and joined right in the conversation. Jewel said, "That sounds like a wonderful idea to me."

Oscar and Sam raised their arms and began to dance and sing their ice cream song, "Mmmmm, Mmmmm, ice cream, yeah! Everyone screams for ice cream!" They laughed and thanked Mama for the great news.

Mama Hannah quickly realized she had never asked Bubba if she could take their children on an outing. Since she suggested the ice cream party, she felt it was important to ask his permission. The next day she called Victoria. "Hello Victoria, this is Hannah. I am calling to ask if it would be okay for me to pick up the children so they can have ice cream with my children. I think it's time they met."

"Hannah, that sounds like a great idea. I will ask Bubba, then give you a call back to let you know. I do not see it being a problem."

"Okay, I will wait for your call."

To Hannah's surprise, things worked out as she had planned. Victoria had called and told her Bubba said the kids could go with her and her children to get ice cream. When she drove into the driveway, Oscar, Sam, and Jewel were peeking out the car window to see their new sisters and brothers standing at the door of their big house. Sissy, Big Bro, Jacob, and Lillie were eagerly waiting. Mama Victoria waved and opened the door to let them go to the car. Mama Hannah instructed Sissy to sit in the front with her since she was the oldest. The other three joined their new sister and brothers in the back seat. Mama Victoria was still standing at the door with a big smile on her face. *"So, this is what a blended family looks like,"* she thought.

This was the first time Hannah and Victoria witnessed all the children together. They were making history. Mama Hannah told Victoria they would not be very long. They waved goodbye.

As soon as the car pulled off, the kids started chatting away with excitement to each other. Mother Hannah realized she did not get a chance to introduce them, but she did not want to interrupt their fun. They seemed so happy. Soon, Mama Hannah arrived at a nearby park and pulled in the closest space. The ice cream truck was not far. Everyone got out of the car. Mama Hannah treated the children to what they wanted. They got in line to get their favorite ice cream. There were serval benches close by to sit on. Mama Hannah said, "After you get your ice cream, go sit on the benches." All the children were enjoying talking to each other while eating their ice cream. They were really enjoying themselves. She did not have the heart to stop them from talking in order to have them tell each other their names. Her heart filled with joy just watching them getting along so well and so quickly.

Mama Hannah overheard Sissy, Lillie, and Jewel talking about living together. They seemed excited about living together. They joined hands and started jumping for joy. The boys were off to the other side, mingling getting acquainted. After a while, Mama Hannah pointed to her watch to let the kids know it was time to leave. She had told Mama Victoria she would not be gone long.

After leaving the park, Mama Hannah drove the kids home and pulled into the driveway. The children were still talking and laughing.

"Okay, okay, did everyone enjoy their ice cream?" Mama Hannah said, smiling.

All the children said in unison, "Yes, thank you."

Mama Hannah got out of the car and escorted Sissy, Big Bro, Jacob, and Lillie to the door. Mama Victoria was holding the door open to welcome them back home. Their faces were sad because they were not ready to stop having fun with their new brothers and sister.

"What is the matter?" Both Mama Hannah and Mama Victoria said.

"We want to go with you, Mama Hannah!" Sissy said.

"You will very soon, Honey. The time is getting close. You have to be patient," Mama Hannah said lovingly.

Victoria told Hannah that Bubba agreed that the girls could go live with her as soon as school was out. Hannah was so excited. Before long, they were all going to become one big, happy, blended family. She prayed this would work out the way she had dreamed.

Even though the children were Hannah's and Bubba's, they had never had a single discussion about the kids going to live with Hannah. Victoria had been the go-between-person and mediator to help make this happen. Victoria and Bubba had never visited Hannah's home or met her new family, but they knew that she would take care of the children.

CHAPTER 11
THE BIG DAY

W hen the day finally came, it was truly a miracle from God. It was a very special day, so waking up early was important to everyone. It was a school day, and Mama Hannah saw to it that Jewel, Oscar, and Sam were on time for school. Daddy Matthew had already gone to work. Mama Hannah had the house to herself. As she walked through the house humming, she made all the last preparations for Sissy and Lillie to come live with her. You would have thought she was going to church. Her shoes were polished, clothes were laid out the night before, and she even chose a hat for the occasion. Mama Hannah felt so good that this day had finally come, and she wanted to look her best. She took one last look at herself before leaving. God had, at last, answered her prayers, and she wanted to show him her gratitude. As she went toward the kitchen door to leave, she noticed Jewel had put treats on the table for Sissy and Lillie when they arrived to welcome them. This made Hannah smile.

Fifteen minutes later, Hannah pulled into Bubba's driveway. Victoria opened the door when she saw Hannah's car pull up. "Come on in and have a seat. The kids are almost ready." Hannah sat in the chair while she waited for the girls.

Sissy rushed around the house to make sure she did not forget any of her personal things. Lillie followed Sissy just like a younger sister does. No suitcases were packed because they did not have one—and they had never traveled before, so they did not need luggage. When they finished, all their belongings were stuffed in two nice gym bags that Mama Victoria had given them for this special occasion. They stood waiting for Mama Hannah to finish talking to Big Bro and Jacob. They were ready to go.

"I am so sorry, but you cannot come live with me right now, Big Bro and Jacob. Your dad did not give me permission to take you with me." The boys were sad but did not seem too disappointed.

Mama Victoria knew this day would come, so she braced herself. Tears were welling up in her eyes, but she was determined not to let them fall. She wanted this to be a great day. Mama Victoria, Big Bro, and Jacob stood in the doorway as Mama Hannah, Sissie, and Lillie walked towards them.

"Do not be sad; we will see you very soon, okay?" Sissy said to her brothers.

The children hugged each other. Big Bro and Jacob watched as Sissy and Lillie put their bags in Mama Hannah's car. Sissy sat in the front while Lillie climbed in the back. The boys waved as the car backed out of the driveway. Nothing was said between Big Bro, Jacob, and Mama Victoria. They knew the house would be quieter because Sissy and Lillie did most of the talking.

Such a relief had overcome Sissie and Lillie. They had never felt what it would be like to live with their birth mother. Finally, they knew their wish was coming true. They were so excited they felt butterflies in their stomach.

Mama Hannah's feelings were different from Sissie and Lillie's feelings. She felt a part of her was being put together with having her girls with her, but another part was still torn from her heart because she could not take her boys with her. It took her a minute to compose herself before she started the car to drive off. Mama Victoria, Big Bro, and Jacob were still standing in the doorway watching. Mama Hannah wanted so badly to tell her sons to grab their bags and come with her, too. But she knew it would cause problems with Matthew and Bubba if she had.

"How did I put myself in such a predicament?" Hannah asked herself as a tear escaped her eyes. She glanced to see if Sissie saw her crying as she brushed the tear away, but Sissy was busy looking out her window. Hannah felt the deep pain that took her back to the day she walked away from Daddy Bubba. She had thought, one day, this feeling would be gone, but she now understood that pain would never go away until the day Big Bro and Jacob could join them.

"Are you all ready to go?" Mama Hannah said, trying to sound cheerful.

"Yes."

Sissy sat quietly. She had waited anxiously for this moment. She did not know she would be speechless. The look on Mama Victoria and her brothers' faces took her breath away. It was as though they were never going to visit again. Lillie was sitting in the backseat, waving goodbye to her family, but she did not know if she should be happy or sad. Mama Hannah pulled off and headed home.

The girls were talking with excitement, which eased the pain for Mama Hannah leaving Big Bro and Jacob behind. The drive was not too far. She pointed out landmarks to prepare the girls for going back and forth to their old and new homes. Lillie recognized their school, and the conversation about it caused Mama Hannah to be filled with joy. Sissy was getting anxious, asking how much further they had to go. Mama Hannah assured her not far at all. She made a few more turns and then said, "Okay, this is our street girls. Do you want to guess which house it is?"

Both Sissy and Lillie guessed the wrong house. Almost at the other end of the block is when Mama Hannah turned into the driveway. The girl's eyes became big.

They said almost simultaneously, "Mama Hannah is this your home?"

It seemed like an Eternity for this day to have come. She took a deep breath with a big smile on her face and then said, "No, this is our home. This is where you will be living now."

Sissy could hardly wait for the car to stop before trying to get out.

Mama Hannah shrieked, 'Wait, Sissy, slow down!"

As she parked the car and the three of them got out, they gathered their bags and went into the house. Jewel was waiting for them in the living room. She hugged then held their hands to lead them to their bedroom. Daddy Matthew was sitting waiting for an introduction, but they had quickly passed him by. Mama Hannah's face explained how she felt. There was no need to ask any questions. He had never seen her face light up so bright.

That look did not last too long after Mama Hannah sat down to explain to Daddy Matthew how the journey had gone. The more she talked, he could see she was saddened she had to leave Big Bro and Jacob behind. She told him about the girl's enthusiasm from the time they were picked up until getting out of the car.

"Well, I can believe every bit of it because they walked right past me. Jewel grabbed them by the hand and went off into the bedroom," Daddy Matthew said with disappointment in his voice.

After Mama Hannah heard the news, she knocked on the girl's door then opened it. She said, "Jewel, I need you to go back into the living room and apologize to your dad for being rude. Sissy and Lillie, I need you to follow her."

Jewel did as she was told. "Dad, I apologize for being rude and not introducing my sisters to you."

He said, "I know you are excited, so your apology is excepted."

"Dad, these are my sisters, Sissy and Lillie. Sissy and Lillie, this is my dad. Well, our dad, since you live here, too."

They walked towards him, and he reached out to hug them. "I'm glad the two of you have joined our family," he said with a big smile on his face.

Sissy and Lillie felt even more welcomed.

Mama Hannah asked the girls if they wanted the snacks Jewel left on the table for them. She started preparing dinner then asked Sissy, Lillie, and Jewel if they wanted to help. Jewel was used to helping her mom in the kitchen, but Sissy and Lillie were not. Mama Victoria never asked them to help prepare dinner. She seemed to have enjoyed being alone in the kitchen. Jewel assured them it would be fun, so they agreed.

"Would you all like burgers and fries for dinner?" Mama Hannah asked.

Everyone said, "Yes!" Jewel had helped before, so she told Sissy and Lillie what they needed to do. It did not take long to complete the dinner with everyone helping. Then, they placed all the plates and utensils on the table.

Jewel usually went to get her brothers to come inside to eat. She knew they were in the neighborhood somewhere playing. Her sisters went with her to go look for Oscar and Sam. As they were looking, Jewel saw some of her friends. She stopped long enough to introduce Sissy and Lillie to them. Then she spotted her brothers and yelled, "Brothers, it's time to come inside to eat."

When Oscar saw Jewel and his two new sisters, he ran fast as he could toward them. Sam had not noticed his sisters, but he ran fast behind his brother. They all hugged one another before going inside. Jewel was the leader as they walked inside the house to the bathroom. It was a line of five children waiting to wash their hands. Jewel told everyone where they would be sitting, and she helped Mama Hannah fix the plates. Daddy Matthew was sitting at the table watching and listening to everything. It was amazing for him to watch what he thought would not work. So far, having a blended family was not too bad, he thought.

Jewel and Mama Hannah joined the family to eat their first meal together. Sissy and Lillie were watching to see why everyone was quiet. They had their heads bowed, so Sissy and Lillie did the same. Daddy Matthew prayed over the food and thanked God for all of them being together as a family. While eating, they discussed various topics. Lillie was quieter than the other children because she was focused on enjoying her dinner. When they finished their meal, Mama Hannah told Jewel to help Sissy and Lillie get cleaned up before going to bed. Oscar and Sam helped Mama Hannah clean the kitchen. All the children went to bed. The house was quiet.

"One day down," Daddy Matthew said as he hugged Hannah. "I told you it would work out."

CHAPTER 12
THE JOY AND PAIN OF CHANGE

ama Hannah took all the children to school the next day. Sissy and Lillie needed a guardian to escort them since it was their first day. Jewel told everyone where they should meet after school. Jewel, Oscar, and Sam knew where their classes were, so they all hugged and went their separate ways. Mama Hannah went into the office with Sissy and Lillie to make sure all their enrollment papers were completed. Mama Hannah hugged the girls and told them she hopes they have a great day, then left. A school escort was waiting to show them where their classes were.

Sissy was able to make new friends because she never met a stranger. Whereas Lillie being a follower, found it hard to meet friends on her first day. Some of her classmates wanted to get to know her, but she was too shy to mingle. After school, Jewel waited for everyone to meet up in the location she had told them earlier. One by one, they all arrived and were soon ready to leave. Jewel, Oscar, and Sam were concerned about how Sissy and Lillie's day went, so they asked. Sissy acted as though it was not a big deal.

Lillie said, "It was weird because no one wanted to talk to me." Everyone assured her it would get better.

Usually, when Jewel, Oscar, and Sam arrived home, Daddy Matthew would be there. Sure, enough he was there on that day waiting for them. The five of them walked into the house, spoke, and gave hugs. Hugging was unusual for Sissy and Lillie, but they caught on quickly. Mama Hannah had not arrived home from work. Jewel and her brothers had a routine they informed Sissy and Lillie about.

Oscar said, "The first thing we do is change clothes, so we will not get our school clothes dirty."

"After changing, we take our book bags to the kitchen table," said Sam.

Eagerly waiting her turn, Jewel said, "Before we do our homework, we get to eat our snack."

Lillie said, "Now that's the best part." They all laughed and agreed.

"What if we do not have homework?" Sissy asked.

Jewel explained, "You have to either make up some or write a letter and show it to Mama Hannah."

Sissy asked, "Write a letter to who?"

"Anyone you wish," Jewel said.

Sissy decided to write a thank you letter to Mama Hannah and Daddy Matthews for letting her and Lillie live with them.

By the time Mama Hannah made it home, the children had finished eating their snacks and were doing their homework. Mama Hannah was very proud of them. They were all getting along and showing they could be responsible. This made her happy. Mama Hannah made their favorite meal for dinner while the kids finished their homework. Later, they got their baths and put out their clothes for school. After watching TV, they said their prayers and went to bed.

Several weeks had passed since Sissy and Lillie came to live with Mama Hannah and Daddy Matthew. Mama Hannah had not taken the children to see Big Bro and Jacob since the big move occurred. Sissy missed her brothers terribly. So asked Mama Hannah when they could go visit. Mama Hannah told her she would contact Daddy Bubba and Mama Victoria to see if it was okay for them to visit.

After a couple of days, Mama Hannah made the call. "Hi, Victoria. How are you and the family?"

"Hi, Hannah. We're fine, thanks."

"We all miss Big Bro and Jacob. The kids need to see each other. When is a good time for us to visit?"

Mama Victoria told her she would check with Daddy Bubba. Each time Mama Hannah heard Daddy Bubba's name, she felt uneasy. Even though she felt nervous about what Bubba might say, as their mother, she had to do what was best for her kids.

Days had passed since Hannah spoke to Victoria. Finally, Victoria called her back, "This Saturday or Sunday would be a good time to visit. Will you be bringing Sissy and Lillie?"

"Yes, I will be bringing all the children," Mama Hannah said with excitement.

Visiting day had arrived, and they got ready to go see Big Bro and Jacob. Mama Hannah told the children to get in the car. Sissy and Lillie were looking at Daddy Matthew, thinking he would come with them. He stood in the doorway waving goodbye.

Sissie asked, "Why doesn't he ever visit?"

Mama Hannah stumbled over her words because she had never been asked that question. Then she said, "It is a complicated situation for children to understand."

While riding, Sissy pointed out to her new siblings all the familiar places. They were impressed that Sissy knew the area so well.

Mama Victoria was standing at the door with a big smile on her face when they arrived. She was happy to see everyone, especially Sissy and Lillie. When they got out of the car, Sissy and Lillie ran to give Mama Victoria a great big hug. They went inside to look for Big Bro and Jacob.

Mama Victoria said, "The boys went out to play and will be home soon."

Lillie filled up most of the time telling Mama Victoria about all the exciting things that had been going on since they moved. Sissy could not get a word in because everyone was talking at once.

Mama Hannah said to Lillie, "Be nice and save some for Sissy to tell."

So, when Sissy began to talk, she was just as excited as her siblings. The most thrilling news Sissy shared was about her new friends at her new school.

CHAPTER 13
DISAPPOINTMENT

A few hours had gone by, but Big Bro and Jacob had not returned. Mama Victoria had no idea where they had gone to play. Since the boys were teenagers now, they were able to come and go as they pleased. Sissy offered to look for them, but Mama Hannah told her they needed to get back home soon. Mama Hannah and the girls were very disappointed they did not get to see Big Bro and Jacob. She told Mama Victoria she would arrange to visit another time. They all said their goodbyes and left to go home.

Mama Victoria knew that Hannah and the girls' visits to Daddy Bubba's house had become increasingly difficult because the children were older now and had joined different sports teams at school and were hardly at home. Other times, Big Bro and Jacob were usually off doing their own thing. After Sissy and Lillie moved, Daddy Bubba's time at home had decreased considerably. Mama Victoria hardly saw any of them, and it saddened her. But she had become used to the arrangement.

Sissy's transition to her mother's house was successful. She made a lot of new friends in her neighborhood and community over the summer. She was a well-liked young lady. She did not spend as much time with Lillie as she did before, and she missed her brothers. But she was busy dealing with peer pressure to hang out with boys. It was starting to get the best of Sissy. She had begun to walk home and hold hands with someone she considered her boyfriend. She would try to hide this from her sisters, but they saw her a few times, but never told on her.

Lillie and Sissy used to be together all the time when living at Daddy Bubba's house. Since Jewel was in Lillie's life now, she did not mind Sissy going off and leaving her. Jewel had friends who did not know Lillie, but she introduced them to her. But sometimes, Lillie felt left out of some of the activities that were going on in the neighborhood. Nevertheless, their summer was full of interesting activities.

CHAPTER 14
MAJOR TROUBLE

S issy headed straight home from school. She did not want to sneak around with her boyfriend anymore. She thought she was old enough and ready to date since she was in high school–and dating was a big deal to her. She had made up her mind that she was going to do things right and ask for her parents' permission. She was so excited as she walked in the door. "Hi, Mama Hannah and Daddy Matthew. I came straight home from school because I wanted to talk to you about something that is very important to me. I think I am old enough and ready to date. But I did not want to before I had your permission," she said confidently, thinking he would be in agreement with her.

When she finished talking, Daddy Matthew wrinkled his forehead and yelled, "Who told you that you were ready to start dating? You are not ready just because you want to date. You don't know the first thing about dating or what you will be getting yourself into! Before you know it, there will be another mouth to feed! Let me tell you about being ready! You have to show you can be responsible and trustworthy. Start by taking care of the chores that you're supposed to do every day, but you don't. Work on your grades and try doing what we tell you to do. Then we can have a discussion!"

As soon as Daddy Matthew finished, Sissy blurted out, "You have already made up your mind instead of having a conversation about me dating! You did not even ask any questions. Why can't we ever just have a conversation about something without you just saying what you think or feel and never asking what I think."

"We have never had a discussion about dating because you have not shown that you are mature enough to take on the responsibility it takes to date! So, you will not date today or any day as long as you are living in this house and not obeying our rules! You can always go back to live with Daddy Bubba, if you are not going to abide by the rules in this house," he said.

Mama Hannah looked at Daddy Matthew in shock, "Now just wait a minute! Both of you need to calm down so we can have a discussion." She had not talked with Sissy about dating because she thought she had more time. She had no idea Sissy would spring this on them. She knew they were at a crossroad. Things had been said that should not have been said. Hannah wasn't sure if the hurt feelings could ever be repaired.

Daddy Matthew's yelled, "I am not going to put up with any back talk from anybody. Sissy acts like she's reached a point in her life where she no longer has to listen to us. We're her parents!"

Jewel and Lillie arrived home and stopped in the driveway when they heard yelling coming from inside. This was unusual. They looked at each other in shock and rushed into the house. Peeking into the kitchen, they saw Sissy, Mama Hannah, and Daddy Matthew shouting at each other. Everyone was trying to make their point at the same time. Jewel and Lillie did not know what to think, but they knew it would be best not to get in the middle of this confusion. So, they quickly went straight to their bedroom. The walls were thin, so yelling was heard throughout the house.

Sissy shook her head in frustration and glared at Daddy Matthew. She thought Mama Hannah would help her explain to Daddy Matthew that she was ready to date, but Mama Hannah didn't say anything to support her. Sissy went to her bedroom, sat on the bed, and tried to figure out what to do. The conversation did not go the way she thought it would. She decided the best thing for her to do was to leave this house. She gathered a few of her personal belongings and walked to the kitchen.

Mama Hannah saw Sissy with a bag in her hand headed toward the door. She walked behind Sissy, trying to get her to stop and talk about what happened. "Sissy, please don't leave. Can the two of us at least talk about it?" Mama Hannah said frantically.

With tears rolling down her face, Sissy stopped and turned to face Mama Hannah, "There is nothing to talk about. If I continue to live here, I cannot do anything I want to do. I am not a little girl anymore, Mama! Ever since I came to live with you, you treated me like I was as young as the rest of them! I have my own friends, and I am going to date, whether you guys like it or not! I do not think Daddy Matthew wanted me to live here anyway! I do not want to be anywhere I am not wanted! I will be glad to get out of this house." she said as she opened the door to leave.

"Sissy!" Hannah cried out.

"My God! Can't you see I need some space, Mama Hannah? You, Daddy Matthew, Daddy Bubba, and Mama Victoria do not understand how I feel right now! I am hurting inside and have been this way for a long time. I have no one, and I mean *no one* to share my feelings with. Furthermore, I do not think you all care! I thought I was doing you a favor by coming to live with you. After all, you were the one who was looking so sad every time you came to visit us at Daddy Bubba's house. I thought some of your problems would ease up if I came to live with you. From what I have seen, it only seemed to have made things worse. You nor Daddy Matthews have to worry about me coming back to live here. I will be graduating soon anyway, and then I will be living on my own!"

"Sissy, I know. That is why I want the two of us to talk. I know things have not gone the way you thought they should. Once we all cool off and come together to talk, I believe there will be some understanding. Please do not leave like this, Sissy.

At least let me share some things with you. You are not the only one walking around hurting. I know this mess is so confusing, and that is one of the reasons we are all hurting. The only person that can straighten this mess out is God!" exclaimed Mama Hannah as she followed Sissy outside.

Sissy walked down the driveway just as the sun was beginning to set. She knew she should not have left the house without trying to settle things. But she was angry and felt no one understood her. She had made up her mind that she was going to leave. As she walked down the dark streets, her stomach was in knots as she thought about what Mama Hannah had said, *"Only God can straighten out this mess."*

Mama Hannah's heart broke as she watched Sissy walk down the driveway and disappear around the corner. She turned to go back into the house. She was perplexed about what had just happened. When she looked at Daddy Matthew with his head in his hands, he looked sad and broken. He would not make eye contact with her. Mama Hannah felt bad about the whole situation.

Hannah began to worry that she had not made the right decision when she walked away from Bubba and the children. She did not expect the hurt she was experiencing to affect everyone else in her life. But she sees that pain can last a long time and is transferrable. She was so sad that she caused her daughter's pain and her husband's anguish. She wanted so badly to fix this problem.

That night, Hannah could not sleep. She was worried about Sissy since she was so upset when she left and because she had no idea where Sissy might have gone. Hannah finally accepted that she needed help from God because He understands everything we go through. Hannah got on her knees and prayed. She confessed her sins and asked for God's forgiveness. She asked the Lord to guide her and help her right the wrongs she has caused in her family's lives.

Before going to bed, Mama Hannah called Mama Victoria to fill her in on what had happened and to inform her that Sissy might be headed to their house. Mama Victoria thanked her and told her she would tell Sissy to call her and let her know when she arrived safely. Mama Hannah felt relieved and waited by the phone. But the phone never rang!

The next morning, Mama Hannah checked Sissy's room to see if she had returned during the night; but the room was empty. So, she called Mama Victoria to see if Sissy had shown up there, but she had not gone there either. Both women were very concerned now.

Three days passed, and no one had heard from Sissy. Mama Hannah believed it was only right for her to call Daddy Bubba since Sissy was last in her care. The thought of doing so was stressful because she did not know how Bubba would react. Hannah called to speak to Bubba, but Victoria told her he was not home. Hannah told Victoria she would call Bubba later to speak to him about Sissy.

As soon as Victoria hung up the phone, Sissy walked into the house. "Sissy, you had us worried sick about you. Are you alright? I understand you have been gone for three days," Mama Victoria said. She could see Sissy looked unkempt.

Looking down at the floor, Sissy said quietly, "Yes, I am alright."

Mama Victoria told Sissy she needed to call Mama Hannah to let her know because everyone was concerned.

"No one cares about me or how I feel. I was trying to tell them, and they did not want to listen. I am not the one that needs to call them." Sissy snapped.

Mama Victoria said, "Sissy, Mama Hannah does care about you and how you feel. She's been worried sick about you. So, if you don't call her, I will. We all care about how you feel, and we want to help if you just talk to us."

"Did Daddy Bubba find out about this?" Sissy said, staring at Mama Victoria. She was hoping the news had not gotten to him yet, because he would usually blow things out of proportion.

"If you had not shown up when you did, he would have been the next person I was going to call." Mama Victoria was very careful with her words, but she knew it was important to let Sissy know what she did was unacceptable.

Sissy began to open up to Mama Victoria, "I promise I will not act like that again. I was mad and wanted my way. So, I wanted them to hurt like I was hurting. But I learned a lot in those three days away from home. Roaming the streets is nothing I want to ever experience again. Moving back with you guys is what I decided I want to do."

"But I thought you wanted to live with Mama Hannah. That was something you have wanted to do for so long, and now you have changed your mind? I do not understand what is going on, Sissy. Please explain it to me," Mama Victoria said, putting her hands on her hips.

"Well, I want to date because I am old enough to have a boyfriend! Plus, all the rest of my friends are dating. I asked Daddy Matthews and Mama Hannah if I could date because I was trying to do the right thing by getting their permission first. But it blew up in my face. They got mad and didn't want to listen. We never had a real conversation. We all got mad and were talking at the same time. Daddy Matthews told me if I was not going to follow the rules in his house, I could go back where I came from. I did not want to hear what they had to say anymore, so I left. And that was that!" Sissy sounded relieved, as if a load was lifted off her shoulders.

"Sissy, your Daddy has rules for everyone living in this house as well," Mama Victoria reminded her. "This will always be your home. But things have changed since you and Lillie left. Daddy Bubba is hardly ever home, and since Big Bro and Jacob are older, they are gone a lot, too. But when everyone is here, they are expected to do what Daddy Bubba tells them and follow the rules. Having rules doesn't mean you don't love or care about someone. I will let Daddy Bubba know you are back at home. Now, go get some rest. I'm sure you're tired."

Walking down the hall towards her bedroom, it was just as Mama Victoria had said. The house was quiet. Sissy went to her room that she used to share with Lillie. This was the first time she would have the bedroom to herself. She lay across the bed thinking about all that had happened over the past several days. It was truly an eye-opener. Sissy was trying to make sense of it all, but it did not come together clearly. She was very hurt by what happened at Mama Hannah and Daddy Matthew's house. The argument started over what she thought she wanted. They said they wanted to train her into what they considered to be a respectable young lady. That is not how Sissy saw it. She thought they just wanted to boss her around and not let her live her life.

Sissy had a hard time falling asleep. She knew Mama Victoria was going to tell Daddy Bubba about what happened at Mama Hannah's house and how she stayed in the streets for three days. Sissy did not know when or how it was going to happen, but she braced herself for her dad's wrath.

The next morning, Sissy walked into the kitchen and saw Daddy Bubba sitting at the table drinking coffee. When he saw her, he got up and left. Sissy suspected Mama Victoria had told him about what happened because he did not say anything to Sissy. This hurt Sissy because it made her feel as if he did not care about her either. Because if he did, he would have at least reprimanded her about leaving Hannah's house and not telling him and staying gone for three days. For the next three days,

After Sissy moved back home, she started acting like she was an adult and was pretty much on her own. She began dating without asking anyone's permission. Daddy Bubba never complained about her dating, nor did he say how he felt about it. So, Sissy felt like it must be alright, or he would tell her if it wasn't. Thinking back to when she lived with her mother, she had no idea dating could cause so much confusion. It saddened her to think her relationship with Mama Hannah and Daddy Matthew may never be the same after their explosive argument about dating.

Sissy lay across the bed and thought about the morning Mama Hannah had left them. She watched her brothers, sister, and Daddy Bubba cry. Sissy was determined not to let one tear fall. Being strong for them made her even tougher because what they were all going through was unbearable pain. She could not understand why her mother would leave them. Sissy knew she needed help dealing with this whole situation. She recalled when she was a little girl that she heard adults talking about God. But her first experience talking to him was not until her mother left home. God got her through that tough time. Sissy did not tell anyone about the conversation she had with God that morning; it was their secret.

When Sissy left Mama Hannah's home, she did not know where she was going to stay. So, she drifted from one friend's house to another. It was something she did not want to ever experience again in life. That night was frightening! Sissy remembered being afraid as she walked around one dark corner after another, being frightened by the shadows cast along the streets as well as the scary animal sounds in the distance. God helped her make it through those nights. But the last words Mama Hannah said echoed in her mind, *"God will have to fix this confusion."* So, Sissy decided to take a moment to talk to God again.

"I know you have heard my prayers," Sissy said, "because you have delivered me many times from myself. I know you know my name and know everything about me. I know you are a friend to me. I thought I wanted to date when I was at Mama Hannah and Daddy Matthew's house, but I am not sure anymore. I know I should have listened and not reacted the way I did. I said some things I cannot take back, but so did they. This is why I am back here with Daddy Bubba and Mama Victoria.

Thank you for answering my prayers to live with Mama Hannah and allowing me to get to know her. I realize my selfishness caused my family a lot of unnecessary problems. After Mama Hannah abandoned me, well, us, I was still bitter, but wanted to be with her. I thought things could be different if we got to know each other better. Because I was still hurting from being abandoned, I did not give her a chance. I did not give myself a chance to heal. I do not know how to let go of this pain! I do not want to carry it any longer. I know there is power in the name of Jesus! Please, Lord, forgive me for carrying the hurt that I should have given to you long before now."

Thinking back over the years, tears began to flow down Sissy's face. Tears slid down her cheeks as she thought about being without her mother when she was young. She also thought about how much Daddy Bubba was hurt when Mamma Hannah left their family. Tears flowed for when she wanted to leave and go home with Mama Hannah each time she visited. Tears flowed for when she walked the streets at night alone, thinking she had nowhere to go. Tears flowed because she and Lillie had not talked for a long time. Tears flowed because of the disconnection she had with her family, and tears flowed thinking no one loved her. Sissy had never emptied herself like she had on that day in her room. She was hoping when she finished praying that God would speak to her because she knew without a doubt, He was listening to her. Sissy cried uncontrollably and balled up in a knot on her bed, clinching her stomach, pouring out to the Lord. She had become tired and weary of the pain she had been trying to cover up and manage on her own.

God patiently waited for Sissy to finish her heartfelt prayer before talking to her. He wanted Sissy to understand that she needed his Son, Jesus, to live a life that would be pleasing to him. He also wanted her to be obedient to her parents and follow their rules because He had given a commandment to all children to honor their mother and father. But Sissy was having a hard time doing this. He wanted her to know that if she followed His commandments, she would live a long life. His plan for her life could not be fruitful if she continued to carry anger, disappointment, and frustration about her past. God told her to give him all the burdens she had been carrying around for way too long. Sissy could be set free from bondage if she surrendered and asked to be forgiven for her past sins. Sissy cried out in anguish as she lay on her bed.

The Lord spoke to Sissy, *"Thank you for coming to me once again. You do know you can come to me as often as you want. I have been waiting on you all along. I need you as much as you need me, Sissy. I heard you confess to your sins, and I understand how much you are hurting. But before I can help you heal, you must surrender by asking to be forgiven. Your healing will come through your surrendering. You are waiting for your family to say they are sorry for what they did. But they have already asked my forgiveness for what they have done. I have talked to them and told them what they needed to do. Your family has moved on from those episodes—and you must do the same. I am waiting on you, Sissy. The enemy has tricked you into thinking there is no need for you to surrender. You have broken our fellowship because you have not surrendered. I am here, Sissy. I can handle your pain. Give it to me. I did not* create you to carry the load you are carrying. Please put your trust in me like you have before. You have nothing to prove to anyone. Your life will be so much brighter and joyful. Today is your day, Sissy. Yesterday is gone, and tomorrow is not promised. No one can make a choice for you."

CHAPTER 15
MISSING YOU

The love Lillie received from her family was what she needed at the time. Daddy Matthew and Mama Hannah continued to treat her the same as they did when she first came to live with them. Her sister, Jewel, already had friends, and her brothers were always together. Lillie was shy but made friends at the new church they attended. There were many activities for the youth, and it was a lot of fun. But even though Lillie was going to church and was active with the youth ministries, she felt something was missing.

Before they moved to Mama Hannah's house, Sissy would take Lillie everywhere–the two were inseparable. When Lillie learned to walk, she tried to keep up with her big sister. She went to live with Mama Hannah because Sissy wanted to go, and she did not want to be separated from her big sister. But, when Sissy decided to move back to Mama Victoria and Daddy Bubba's house, Lillie did not go. Even though there would be a void and she would miss her, Lillie wanted to stay with Mama Hannah. She often wondered why her relationship with her sister had to end just because of Sissy's fallout with Mama Hannah and Daddy Matthew.

Lillie often thought about how home and church would be different if Sissy were still around. She wished she could have talked to Sissy before she left. She had no idea that day would be the last time she would see or speak to Sissy. Lillie wanted to hear Sissy's side of the story. She never heard Mama Hannah or Daddy Matthew's side of the story either. They acted as if nothing had happened. Usually, Lillie would overhear conversations about people, but she didn't hear anything about Sissy. She and Jewel would periodically talk about their personal opinions about what happened, but that is as far as it went. Things did not turn out the way she thought they would. Otherwise, Sissy would still be living with them. It saddened Lillie to think that she had not seen or talked to Sissy in a long time.

CHAPTER 16
WHO COULD IMAGINE

U nlike Sissy, Lillie decided not to ask anyone's permission to date. The memory of Sissy, Daddy Matthew, and Mama Hannah yelling at each other just because Sissy wanted to date made Lillie avoid the topic altogether, especially since Daddy Matthew made it clear that dating was not allowed in his home. Even when Lillie thought it would be best to talk with them, she decided not to because she did not believe they could have a civil conversation about dating.

Lillie was excited that she was in her last year of middle school. Before school, during lunch, and after school, Lillie noticed that everyone seemed to be cuddled up with someone. She was feeling the peer pressure to hook up with someone, too. She had no desire to go against the rules Daddy Matthew had established, but she wanted to have someone special in her life just like the other girls did. So, Lillie began sneaking around, talking on the phone to a male friend. This male had one thing on his mind—and several times when he and Lillie were together, he achieved his goal. All through her school years, Lillie was a quiet follower. At home and in church, she was taught to have self-respect and behave like a young lady. Lillie wanted to have self-control, to be more vocal, and strong. But she did not exhibit any of these characteristics.

When two months passed and Lillie had not had her monthly cycle, she knew she was in a tough predicament. Because of not saying "no" or speaking up for herself, she found herself having an unplanned pregnancy. Dating and having sex was not a topic that was discussed in her household. When Daddy Matthew told Sissy she could not date, it was his way of telling her he did not want her to bring a baby into their home. Now Lillie understood why Sissy was not given permission to date and why the discussion got so heated.

"Oh, my God, I pray I am not pregnant?" Lillie thought to herself every day. She did not want to have to say this prayer. Lillie had no one she could talk to about her situation. If Sissy were still living with them, maybe, just maybe, she would have spoken to her. But right now, Lillie felt all alone, even though she was around other people.

Since it was cold outside, Lillie was able to keep her growing stomach covered with bulky sweaters and coats. When the season changed, she could not hide it much longer. Once Lillie removed the layer of clothing, she knew the world would know what she had been doing in the dark. It would be a surprise to some and a tragedy to others. No, she could not be pregnant! It would be too embarrassing for Lillie and her family. What would both sets of her parents say? Lillie had three more years of high school ahead of her. How can I finish school with a baby?

Lillie's thoughts about possibly being pregnant seemed to occupy her mind full-time. "If I am pregnant and the word gets out, everyone will say, 'I thought she was a quiet, innocent girl. Out of sight, out of mind. This is the consequence of having intercourse without protection and being dishonest. When the little one grows on the inside, the outside grows as well. Not only does the stomach grow, so does everything else." Then Lillie entertained a childish thought, *"If I do not think about the pregnancy, it will go away."*

One evening, Lillie walked past Mama Hannah to go to her bedroom. Mama Hannah stopped abruptly and glanced hard at Lillie. "Girl, you are gaining weight. You are not pregnant, are you?" she asked.

Lillie continued walking down the hall as if she had not heard her mother. But her ears could not ignore her anymore as Mama Hannah said those dreaded words again, even louder, "Lillie! You are not pregnant, are you?"

"Yes, I think so," Lillie said quietly. "I have not had my monthly cycle for a while."

Mama Hannah's countenance appeared as if someone had sucked all the life out of her. Her shoulders drooped as she looked at the floor, shaking her head side-to-side. It was clear that she was not ready to hear this news. She walked slowly to the kitchen and sat at the table. She took several deep breaths and dropped her head in her hands. "Lillie, baby, please come have a seat. Do you know what you have done to your life, little girl? I cannot begin to tell you the opportunities you will miss out on still being a child yourself. I know your father nor Daddy Matthew will take this too well at all," Mama Hannah said as she looked at Lillie for a long while. "You will need to tell Daddy Matthew," as she got up from the table and left the room.

Lillie's heart began to race. *What will Daddy Matthew think? What will he say?* She felt awful knowing that once Daddy Matthew finds out, he might put her out of the house like he did Sissy. I know he's going to be so mad at me, Lillie thought. She tensed up when Daddy Matthew and Hannah walked into the kitchen.

"Tell him, Lillie," Mama Hannah said.

As Lillie began to talk, tears flowed down her cheeks. "Daddy Matthew, I need to tell you something. I don't want to tell you, but I know you need to know." She cried even harder before the words finally came out, "I am pregnant," she said, looking up tearfully at Daddy Matthew. The room fell silent. No one said a word or moved.

Mama Hannah braced herself because she had no idea how Daddy Matthew would react. Daddy Matthew did not say a word as he stared at Lillie in disbelief. Then, he looked at

Hannah, shook his head, left the kitchen, and returned to his bedroom.

Seeing Daddy Matthew just turn and walk away was even scarier than what Hannah or Lillie expected. They had braced themselves to hear him yelling and screaming or pounding on the table. Yet, that was not what happened. Instead, the house was eerily quiet the rest of the night.

The next day after school, Lillie dreaded going home. She was not sure what would happen since Daddy Matthew had all day to think about what he would say to her. She slowly opened the door to the house. Daddy Matthew and Mama Hannah were waiting for her. Lillie's stomach felt like it was in knots. They told her to sit down because they needed to talk with her about her pregnancy. She sat down and listened.

Daddy Matthew began, "First and foremost, having an abortion is not an option. Taking care of the baby while you're in school will be our responsibility. But, as soon as you get home, you have total responsibility for taking care of your child since you created this situation. Finally, there will not be a second child brought into my house. Lillie, if you get pregnant again, you will have to leave this house and move somewhere else." They did not tell her where she had to move, but it was clear she could not live with them and be disobedient.

"Lillie, do you understand?" Hannah asked.

"Yes. I do. Thank you both for agreeing to help me and letting me continue to stay here. I am glad you'll be able to help with the baby when it's born so I can finish school," Lillie said. "This really means a lot to me."

Two years passed with Lillie going to school and managing to take care of her toddler. Her life was filled with more business than any sixteen-year-old girl could handle. Lillie enrolled in a career program at a school for girls who had started families. The program was designed for a student to go to school part-time and work part-time. Having her own money enabled her to do more as she matured into a responsible young lady.

However, Lillie and another guy met on the job and became friends. After a while, their friendship grew into an affair. During the time she was engaging in her affair, she heard Daddy Matthew and Mama Hannah's voices reminding her about her responsibilities and their rules. After a few months, Lillie realized she had missed her monthly cycle. She was devastated. How did she manage to get pregnant again with all that was going on in her life? The words Daddy Matthew told her two years ago rang loudly in her ears. "*Do not have another baby while you're living in this house.*" What would they say? She was only in the second semester of her junior year in high school. She knew Mama Hannah and Daddy Matthew would not handle this situation very well, but she knew she had to tell them.

One evening after school, Lillie broke the news to them. Daddy Matthew glared at her and shook his head in disappointment. "How could you do this again? Well, I told you if you had another baby, you can't live here. So, you're going to have to find another place to live, and you can start looking tonight." The time of day did not matter to Daddy Matthew. Once his rules were broken, there was no getting him to change his mind.

Mama Hannah was disappointed and had nothing to say because Lillie knew the rules. But she was still her child, and she had to help her. Mama Hannah knew she had to pray and ask God to work a miracle for Lillie. She prayed in the quiet of her spirit. Later, she picked up the newspaper and began to thumb through the rental section. HALLELUJAH! He answered her prayers that night! Luckily, Lillie did not have much to move. Mama Hannah thought she would have an evening to rest, but instead, she helped Lillie move into her two-bedroom apartment with her first baby and her second one in her stomach.

Being in her own place was a new adventure for Lillie. She was still in her senior year of high school, had two children, and was not married. But she was doing the best she could under the circumstances; however, her actions made it appear like her parents had not raised her properly. This was an embarrassing time for Lillie and her parents, who had tried to raise her right. Nevertheless, Lillie had her second healthy baby and was still able to graduate with her high school class. She was so proud of herself– raising two children while going to high school. It was very challenging, but Lillie did it!

The fathers of Lillie's two children had no interest in marrying her, and she had no interest in marrying them either. Of course, it should have been an honor for either of them to marry the mother who gave birth to their child. However, they still wanted to run the streets and hang out with the fellas. Lillie was very thankful to have had her children and grateful they had a place they could call home. But she felt lonely. She needed someone to help care for her and the children, but she was unsure what to look for in a man, what to expect from a man, or what a genuine relationship looks like. Lillie did not have any role models. Unfortunately, she had never seen her fathers and mothers be affectionate towards one another. That is just how it was. After having fallen into sin, she wanted something more out of life with a man, not just sex and babies. But if having a special man in her life is not what God wanted for her at the time, she was content with her small, yet big family of three.

Marriage was not a thought or a big deal for Lillie. Sadly, to say, as she continued experiencing life, she also continued to experience toxic relationships.

Chapter 17
Diamond in the Rough

L illie was sitting, waiting patiently for her appointment. She had signed up for a six-week refresher typing course.

A young man walked over to where Lillie sat. "Excuse me," he said, "Lillie, how are you today?"

"I am doing fine Kevin, thanks for asking. How about you?"

"I am fine, thank you for asking. I have a relative who is here visiting. I would like for you to meet him. Is it okay to invite him over?"

"Well, I am waiting to be called into my meeting. You will have to hurry up, though."

Kevin motioned for Jabez to come over. Jabez walked over to where they were.

"Lillie, please meet Jabez, and Jabez, this is Lillie. You guys are adults, so you can take it from here. I have work to do." Kevin started walking out of the office.

"I guess you are going to leave us hanging just like that, huh, Kevin?" Jabez said. Kevin waved goodbye. Jabez looked at Lillie. "How long have you been going to school?"

Lillie was avoiding eye contact because she was shy and felt uncomfortable since she had just met him. "I have not started yet. I have an appointment to talk to someone shortly. I guess they will let me know."

"I am hoping it will go well because I would like to get to know you better, and I will know where to find you. I hope to see you around," he said and walked out of the office.

Lillie was not sure what to think. She had made too many mistakes with men in the past, which made her uninterested in any relationship right now. Finally, her name was called. Lillie's appointment lasted for an hour. After that, the counselor told her she could ride home on the small school bus, if she needed it. She explained to Lillie that transportation was provided to assist their clients in getting to and from school was a bonus for both the agency and their students.

When Lillie finished meeting with the counselor, she walked down the steps to the spot where she could catch the bus. Before boarding the bus, she politely asked the driver if he could stop at the sitter's house so she could pick up her two children on the way home.

"Yes, I sure can," he responded kindly. He had to take Lillie, the new guy, and some other clients to their destinations.

Lillie took a seat on the left side of the bus, two rows behind the driver. The new guy sat on the right side of the bus two rows behind her. She felt him staring at her. She glanced back and saw him gazing and not saying a word. This made her uncomfortable because most of the other riders had already been dropped off. Lillie got off the bus at the sitter's house. She returned with her two bundles of joy and their bags. It was not long before the driver stopped at her destination. Lillie had difficulty getting off the bus. She was small in stature and struggled to carry her baby, the school bag, the diaper bag, and make sure her three-year-old did not fall.

The new guy said, "Miss, may I help you? Please, let me help!"

Before Lillie knew it, she blurted out, "Oh, you can talk now?" she snapped. Then with a smile, she said, "Sure, I would be very thankful if you would."

The new guy took the two bags and held on to the three-year-old's hand, and paused when he saw Lillie stop a few feet from the steps.

"Thank you for helping us. I can handle it from here. By the way, I apologize for snapping at you earlier. But when you were staring at me, it made me feel uncomfortable." She said in a soft yet firm voice.

As he walked to the bus, he turned and said, "Your apology is accepted, but I could not help but stare at the beauty God created for me to see."

Throughout the evening, Lillie's mind kept flashing back to how quiet yet caring her new acquaintance was. She remembered when they were introduced, and she was preoccupied mentally getting prepared for her appointment. Lillie acted as if her appointment was more important than meeting Jabez, but it was not. Instead, just the thought of him gave her butterflies. That was strange since they had not really talked.

Lillie thought about him off and on over the weekend. *"It was interesting that Kevin chose to introduce me to his relative. I am probably the newest girl at the school. Jabez seemed like he was waiting to be in my presence."* She wishes she had written his phone number down so she could call. Waiting until after the weekend to see him again would really test her patience. She let out a big sigh.

When Monday came, she had hoped to see him again at school, but he was not there. She was not sure if he was a student. Lillie did not want anyone to know she was concerned about his whereabouts, so she did not ask. The whole week had gone by, and no new guy. Lillie had overheard a conversation with two people mentioning that the bus driver and Jabez were brothers. She was too shy to ask his brother what his name was and why he had disappeared. She had no information on him, so she just had to wait. Lillie could not understand why she kept thinking about him.

Week two had come, and her thoughts were the same as the previous week. "Ok, if he is not here today, I need the courage to ask his brother some questions," Lillie thought.

This was one of the most uncomfortable situations she had been in a long time. When she boarded the bus, there were other students already on. She no longer had the courage to ask. She was too shy to ask with listening ears, so she remained quiet. When the driver pulled into the school parking lot, there he was–the new guy was talking to someone. All this time, Lillie had secretly been thinking about him and wanted to see him. Suddenly, she became nervous and wanted to disappear. She was trying her best to get lost in the crowd but glanced to see him watching her. Suddenly their eyes locked.

"Hello, Ms. Lady," he said.

There were a few other young ladies in the crowd getting off the bus, so she acted as though he was talking to one of them but knowing all the time, she wanted to be the one he was speaking to.

He walked up next to her and again said, "Hello, Ms. Lady."

"Hello, I thought you were talking to someone else," Lillie said sweetly.

"Now, why would I do such a thing?" he said, looking down on her because he was so much taller than she was.

Lillie did not answer; she just smiled. He asked her if she remembered his name. Lillie looked off to the side, then up and said, "To be honest, I do not remember."

"Great, that makes two of us!" he said with a loud laugh.

"You do not remember your own name," she said, being sarcastic. "Just kidding, but I do not remember your name."

"You have jokes, I see, but I like it. My name is Jabez Richman, and what is yours?" he asked.

She extended her hand and said, "My name is Lillie Roberts. Pleased to meet you, Mr. Jabez Richman."

"Well, I am glad we at least got that out of the way," he sighed. Lillie sighed, too. It was obvious both of them were nervous.

Lillie started walking towards the building, "Well, Jabez Richman, I'm going to class so I will not be late."

"Hope you enjoy your class, and I will see you later."

They walked in opposite directions. Lillie felt a sense of accomplishment. Finally, she was able to see him and found out his name is Jabez. She felt good they were able to talk without any distractions. As Lillie sat in class trying to focus, she had a huge smile on her face.

Jabez, however, did not go to class. He was talking to the fellas; then he left with them. His friends could tell he was interested in Lillie because he drifted off when they all were talking. One of the guys called his name several times to bring him out of his daydream. "Sorry, Man. But there is something special about that girl, and I am going to find out what it is."

Most of the students were interacting in class while the instructor taught, but Lillie did not talk with anyone. She was in a trance. She knew school should be her priority and that she should be paying attention, but her mind was on Jabez. Lillie was not sure if she was going to see or talk to him after class. They still had not exchanged numbers. If she had arrived at school earlier, maybe they could have. For now, she will have to wait.

After Lillie had gathered her belongings, she rushed out of the classroom to see if Jabez was anywhere in sight. Her heart was beating fast because she really wanted to see him and talk on the way home. Lillie was determined she would have enough courage to talk if he did not. She looked everywhere she thought he might be, but he was nowhere to be found—what a letdown. For someone who acted like he was interested in her, he did not stick around to talk to her after class. As she waited for the bus driver to get the bus ready, her heartbeat slowed down. Lillie tried her best not to let her disappointment show. The driver kept glancing at her through the rearview mirror as if he knew she was disappointed. He did not say anything about

Jabez, and neither did she. He asked Lillie if she needed to pick up the children because she had forgotten to say anything. Lillie nodded her head. She picked up her children and soon arrived home. The driver helped her off the bus.

Lillie went to class each day, hoping to see if Jabez was around, but to no avail. On the last day of the school week, she knew if he had not shown up, she would not see him until the following week. Even though she could not seem to catch up with him, his name continued to be in her thoughts. Lillie made sure she remembered Jabez's name; she did not want to go through the whole introduction again. School was out for the week, and once again, he did not show up. She was disappointed, and her enthusiasm about him began to diminish. Lillie needed to decide to either not be concerned or get courageous to ask his brother about him. She knew she was attracted to him, so trying to convince herself not to think about him was not an option.

As she boarded the bus, she asked his brother, "Where has Jabez been lately?"

"I don't know," he said, hunching his shoulders.

"I was just asking," Lillie said sadly.

A few weeks had passed, and Lillie had not been in contact with Jabez. She decided she was going to treat him just like any other guy. He made her feel like he was not as interested as he implied because he was preoccupied with other business and had not reached out to her. She did not want to pour more into this unsure prospect than need be. The butterfly feelings and heart panting left as quickly as they come.

"Is he a student or not? If so, I wonder what classes he's taking?" If I could find that out, it would save all the unnecessary fretting, she thought to herself.

Then there were days he would show up at school at different times. Lillie guessed he was probably not taking any classes. Showing up at the end of the school day most definitely told her he was not enrolled there. When she would be leaving school, it seemed as if he appeared from nowhere. A couple of times, he would continue to talk with his friends as the bus pulled off. Other times, he would hop on and ride. At the beginning of their friendship, Jabez would not sit with her. Lillie was not about to move where he was. This secret attraction was not good for either of them. Being shy was not getting them anywhere.

Lillie did not need any more confusing male relationships in her life. She wanted to do well in her class and pass with high performance. The class she signed up for was not a full semester course, and she was getting close to the end. She was hoping Jabez would pick up his pace to at least ask her on a date. She knew that would be stretching it a bit much, but at least it was a thought. They did not have the same circle of friends. Sadly, Lillie accepted the fact that once her class was completely over, she and Jabez would not see each other at all.

To Lillie's surprise, the last week of school, Jabez was on the bus when she got on. Not only was she surprised, but all the seats were taken except the one next to him. Was that a lucky coincidence? He got up from his seat to let her sit by the window. Lillie hesitated for a moment before sitting next to Jabez. Looking around, she blushed because everyone seemed to be looking at them.

"Good morning, Ms. Lillie," Jabez said.

As Lillie returned the reply, she looked him straight in the eyes, "Good morning, Mr. Jabez."

Jabez was wondering what was with the stern eye contact. "I apologize for not staying in contact or exchanging phone numbers. I know you saw me a couple of times, and we did not get to talk. Can I make up for lost time?"

Lillie wanted to say more than she did, but people were listening. Gazing out the window, she asked, "What do you mean by that? Even if we exchanged numbers, would that really help?"

"Well, I will give you my number, and in return, you give me yours." Then, he put his arm on top of the seat behind her and leaned in closer.

"Jabez, I do not know you that well to give you my number," Lillie whispered.

He looked at her with those dreamy-looking eyes. The driver parked the bus at school. Everyone began to get off the bus. Lillie and Jabez were the last to get off. She insisted that she was not going to give him her number.

"Will you be riding the bus home this evening?" she asked.

Jabez replied, "I plan on it."

Walking away to go to class, she said, "Well, we will talk more then, ok?"

He agreed.

Jabez and Lillie had made headway in their conversation. She was more at ease this time in class because she knew she would see him later. This was the last week of class. Lillie knew the exam would be at the end of the week, and she wanted to do well. So, her priority was to concentrate and do her best to learn everything. She realized that trying to develop a new relationship while studying for an exam would be difficult. Perhaps, Jabez would have to wait.

There was no need for study groups in her class; the exam was based upon the individual's knowledge. She knew she would have to decide to use the typewriter for the test, but she needed time to practice. Immediately after class, she made arrangements to go to the typewriter lab. It took longer than she anticipated, but the bus driver was waiting on her. When she got on the bus, the only seat available was next to Jabez.

"Imagine that! Was he saving the seat for me?" she thought.

Jabez repeated the courtesy greeting from that morning. He is a gentleman, and she liked that part about him. The only thing that bothered her so far was his inconsistency. The secret feelings Lillie had for Jabez led her to believe he should have acted a certain way toward her. But she realized they had not agreed to be in a relationship.

On the way to pick the children up, he asked her if he could assist this time. She did not refuse. Lillie sat in one seat with her toddler and bags; Jabez let the little guy sit in the seat with him to make sure he was safe.

He picked up the conversation where they left off, saying, "So did you get to think about us exchanging phone numbers?"

Lillie kept her word by not exchanging numbers. She explained to him how new their acquaintance was and how she was a little stressed because of her exam. He seemed to understand. But when they arrived at her building, he once again asked for her number as he helped her get off the bus. At this point, she did not answer at all. Instead of answering, she just thanked him and said goodbye.

Lillie found out Jabez did not take "no" for an answer. There were a few more days left, and he showed up every day before and after school. He started helping her on and off the bus without asking. It was obvious he was making up for lost time. The butterflies returned in her stomach when she would see him or get close to him. Little by little, he would hold longer conversations. He led most of the conversations, so his shyness seemed to have gone away. Lillie did not say much. She discovered that he was the talker, and she was the listener. There were times when the two of them would start to say something at the same time. When that happened, it brought a smile to their faces. They enjoyed their talks on the bus rides to and from school. Both knew that meeting on the bus was getting ready to come to an end.

The day of the final exam was the last day of school. Lillie loved to dress, so she dressed up to feel better while taking the exam. When Jabez saw her, his eyes were big, and his jaw dropped.

Jabez said, "You do know you are beautiful inside and out, right?"

Lillie smiled while doing her best to be professional and keep her composure, but Jabez's words really messed her up and made her feel weak in the knees, causing her to wobble in her heels.

Jabez had begun to feel comfortable in her presence. They were getting off the bus, and he extended his hand to help her off. It was a good thing he did because her knees were knocking because she knew he was staring at her, and she wasn't used to this kind of attention. He wished her well on taking her exam then she went to class. Excited was the feeling she felt for a couple of reasons; she believed she would do well, and she would have more time to develop her relationship with Jabez once she completed her class.

The room was quiet when Lillie entered to take her final exam. It was only her, three other students, and the instructor in the room. To be comfortable, she adjusted herself in her seat and started taking her exam. Lillie was surprised when she had finished before the timer had gone off. She took a deep breath because she felt good about what she had accomplished. Lillie let the instructor know she had enjoyed the class very much and thanked her as she left the room.

Lillie walked down the hallway, thinking since she had finished early, she would have time to talk to Jabez before getting onto the bus. Lillie wished the communication between the two of them would have happened sooner because she did not have a social life outside of school. And she never knew when or where she would see him. She looked in the crowd of people where she thought he would be, but Jabez was not there. Lillie went to another location, but he was not there either. Someone who rode the bus with her noticed her looking around and said, "He left with his friends."

Lillie was heartbroken because the last time that happened, she did not see him for weeks. It was about five minutes before it was time to board the bus. As she was standing, she kept looking all around for him. In the last conversation they had before she went to class, Jabez implied they would see each other when she was finished. He knew it was the last day of school. She was crushed because she did not know where or how to contact him. *"Could this be why he kept pressing me to exchange phone numbers? What if he decides he do not want to have anything else to do with me since I did not give him my number?"* she thought.

The bus driver started the bus. That was not the sound she wanted to hear right then. Lillie let others get on before she did, hoping he would show up as he had on other occasions. She was next to the last one to get on, and still no Jabez. His behavior was very puzzling to her. Lillie could tell the driver was not in a hurry to take off, hoping Jabez would show up for her sake. Looking at his watch, he could not wait any longer and drove off. It was one of the longest rides to the sitter without Jabez sitting next to her. What a disappointment! Lillie was glad she had brought a change of shoes because she knew she did not want to struggle with getting the children on and off the bus. She went in to get them. When she returned, the driver helped her and the kids get on the bus.

Lillie had to come up with something quick before getting off the bus if she wanted to see Jabez again. She sat very still, thinking very hard until she came up with an idea. Making things happen when she wanted them to was something she had to learn. Lillie got a piece of paper from her purse and wrote her name and telephone number on it. This was a time she had to put her trust in Jabez's brother. She had never done anything like this ever in life. When it was time to get off the bus for the last time, she thanked the bus driver for all the times he picked her and the children up. Lillie then asked if he would PLEASE give the piece of paper to Jabez when he saw him again.

"Sure. I don't mind. But to be honest, I don't know when I will see him again."

"It doesn't matter; just make sure he gets that paper, understand?" She said sternly. Not knowing what would happen after that, she left it up to God. But she kept her hopes high.

On the way to park the bus, the driver was going over in his head what Lillie had told him. He even laughed to himself when he repeated it. He was surprised to see Jabez and his friends waiting for him in the bus parking lot.

When the driver approached Jabez, he told him, "I don't know why I am giving you this, but I am going to do as I was told," he chuckled. He pretended to hand the note to Jabez but would snatch it back quickly before Jabez could take it.

Jabez was puzzled as he glanced at the paper in his brother's hand. "What is that? Who is it from?"

Keeping Jabez in suspense, he waved the paper in the air and finally handed it to Jabez. "This is your lucky day, brother."

Before opening it, Jabez said, "What are you carrying on about?"

"It is Lillie, the girl you have been talking to on the bus. She told me to give you her number!" His brother said.

Jabez opened the piece of paper. There was her name and number right before his very eyes. His heart skipped a beat, and his mouth opened. Jabez began to jump and run around with a big smile on his face. He could not believe what his eyes had seen. His friends started laughing when he started jumping and running.

"Oh, my God, I cannot believe this is happening! She gave *you* her number to give to me?" Jabez said as he looked at his brother.

They were all happy for him. They gave him a high five and then gave each other a manly hug.

His brother looked at him seriously and said, "Well, don't you think you need to go ahead and make the phone call?"

"I will, but not until I am alone so I can hear every word she says," Jabez smiled again.

They all laughed and joked about different things, but Jabez was no longer involved in their conversation. His mind was on calling Lillie. He could hardly wait.

CHAPTER 18
THE CALL

Jabez made it to his location and went off to a quiet area. Before he dialed Lillie's number, he said a quick prayer, "Father, you know I need a good woman in my life. If she is the one, please let me know. I do not want to keep going through changes like I have. In Jesus Name Amen." Jabez took a deep breath and cleared his throat. His hands were sweaty from being nervous, but he knew this call had to be made. He dialed her number, and the phone rang. It rang longer than he anticipated, but she finally answered.

Lillie paced around her living room. She had hoped Jabez's brother followed her instructions. Then the phone rang! She put her hand on the phone, then took a deep breath. She was hoping and praying it would be Jabez. When Lillie answered and heard Jabez say, "Hello," she knew she had done the right thing by putting her trust in his brother that day.

"Hello, Jabez. I was waiting for your call," Lillie said.

"Lillie, I am so thankful you gave my brother your number. I am sorry I was not there when you finished your exam. I heard you say you were taking a final, and it was your last day. But I just could not make it to the school to ride with you. Will you please forgive me?"

Lillie, being the mild-mannered person she had always been, said, "Sure, I forgive you. I was fearful I would not ever see you again. I looked everywhere at school, thinking you were still on campus. You told me you would ride home with me, so I was not sure what happened to you."

Jabez, "Let me make it up to you. Let's meet for lunch to celebrate your accomplishments."

Lillie said, "That's nice of you to offer, but I don't know." The thought of dating was uncomfortable for her, almost scary. She had not been on a "real" date in years. She was not ready to share all her personal information with Jabez. And since she gave birth to her sons, she spent most of her time taking care of them. The well-being of her children did not seem to interest the kid's fathers, so she had to do everything for them. It did not leave a lot of time for much else.

Jabez looked at her, puzzled by the hesitation. After all, she had initiated the call. He knew they both really liked each other and wanted to see each other again.

"Jabez, I would feel more comfortable in this relationship if we first talked on the phone so we can get better acquainted. Please, please do not get the impression that I do not want to date you, because I do. If I did not want us to be friends, I would not have given you my number. Please, grant my wish and do this for me," Lillie said.

"I will only do it your way if you promise we can talk as often as possible. I really am interested in becoming a close friend," Jabez said.

Lillie had her hand over her heart as if she were trying to keep her promise to herself. She had gone against some of her promises to herself before. Even though she did not agree to go on a lunch date, they stayed on the phone for hours, getting to know one another better, just as she asked. She listened to the questions he asked and answered them the best she could. Jabez was a good listener, even though he talked more than she did. They seemed to enjoy each other's company on the phone. Lillie told Jabez she needed to seek employment. Before the conversation ended, he gave a sly hint that they should go on a date while she had a break. Lillie ignored the comment because she did not want to be pressured into doing something she was not ready for.

Whatever Lillie set her mind to do, her goal was to complete it. Lillie made a list of potential employers and their phone numbers. Trying to schedule job interviews had become a bit more hectic than she anticipated. She succeeded in scheduling a few interviews. She wrote down the dates and times. She left messages for the ones she could not reach. If this worked out the way she planned, this would be her first full-time job.

The next morning, every time the phone rang, Lillie was hoping it was Jabez. When she did not hear his voice, she was disappointed. She also anxiously waited for a potential employer to call. She needed a job to support her and her sons, but she also wanted a social life with Jabez. She was excited about her life because she was on track with the goals she had planned.

When Lillie talked to Jabez that evening, she told him about her day. He could hear in her voice that she was enjoying the job search. He was happy for her because it was something she really wanted. He wished he could be there with her cheering her on into her next journey. But Lillie had made it clear she did not want to be pressured. Jabez believed his turn would come if he gave her space. So, he decided to go out of town.

After several weeks of interviewing, Lillie landed a promising career. Finally, her expectation of getting hired was behind her. Having employment allowed her to get a car, so she did not have to rely on public transportation, family, or friends. Life seemed to be falling into place, except one element was missing. "Why had Jabez not called her?" She kept wondering if he had lost her number.

One evening Lillie was busy getting dinner ready when the phone rang. An unusual feeling came over her before answering the phone. "Hello," Lillie said.

There was a hesitation from the caller. "Hello, may I speak to Lillie," Jabez said.

Her heart started beating faster than usual when she recognized the voice on the other end of the phone. "This is Lillie," she said with excitement in her voice. She had been waiting to hear from him. "What took you so long to call?"

He said, "I went out of town to take care of business and just returned.

She said, "No worries, I have been busy as well. Lillie acted as though she had not been waiting for his call.

"When can I see you so we can catch up?" Jabez asked.

She was overly anxious to hear those words and to see him. Before answering, Lillie had to pull herself together and not sound like she was desperate. She told herself to breathe and calm down. Then she asked, "When would you like to see me?"

"I would like to see you now if I could," he said. Those words sounded so sweet to her ears, and his voice sounded so soft and lovely. To invite him over right then would have sent the wrong message. So, Lillie told him she couldn't see him today. They discussed possible dates and times and settled on the following weekend. They would have to wait nine days to see each other. Those days would seem like an eternity.

Lillie was feeling anxious about starting a relationship with Jabez. She had so many questions and concerns. She remembered going to church and learning about God when she lived with Mama Hannah. At church, she learned that God listened when his children talked to him. Lillie felt she had no one to talk to about relationships, personal matters, or anything important. Since she had put her babies to bed, she decided this would be a good time to talk to the God she had heard about.

CHAPTER 19
SEEK MY FACE

L illie knelt beside her bed, "I do not know the proper way to address You, but I am going to do my best. It feels a little awkward talking to someone I cannot see, but I'll give it a try.

Years ago, I was passing by my mother's bedroom door one night when I heard her call someone, 'Daddy.' Later, I figured out You were the One she was speaking to. I have also heard people call you Father, but I want to call you Daddy like Mama Hannah does. Do you really know everything like others say you do? I have never met anyone who knows everything.

Well, where should I begin? I guess You know what kind of family I grew up in. We were dysfunctional–I had two sets of parents. I know that no one gets to choose their parents. So, since I had four, I always thought I was special. I thought that was not a bad thing, huh? They all loved me in their own way, and I did not turn out too bad. Was that because you were watching over me?

I was taught that when someone is abandoned, they develop trust issues. I believe that is my situation with Jabez. He is interested in building a relationship with me. Being in a relationship with a man makes me nervous; as a matter of fact, it makes me real nervous. I have no one to talk to about this, so I am hoping you can help. What should I expect from a man who seems to be interested in me? I am a young woman with two young babies. I am not sure if Jabez really wants to be in a serious relationship after he gets to know us. I really need your help because I do not want to be just another woman to this man. I have nine days before we see each other again. If I could hear from you before then, I believe my life will be less nerve-racking. Will you promise to talk to me before then, Daddy?"

Days passed, and Lillie had not heard from God. One day she was at lunch in the break room. Lillie whispered aloud, *"I have not heard from You. Where are You? I asked you not to leave me! The date is getting closer, and I need to know the right thing to do. Please, please say something, anything!"*

A lady sitting across from Lillie looked at her as if to say, *"Who are you talking to?"*

Lillie quickly looked down at her food and began to eat, hoping the lady had not heard her.

The woman saw the worried look on Lillie's face. Anyone who had a caring heart could see something was wrong. The lady got up and went over to Lillie. "I can sense something is bothering you," she said. "Are you okay?"

Lillie was reluctant to tell a stranger her business, but the lady seemed genuinely concerned. They introduced themselves–Diane was the lady's name. She appeared to be older than Lillie. They had seen each other before in the break room but never took time to have a conversation.

Diane apologized for staring at Lillie and interrupting her lunch. To break the ice, she began to share with Lillie about some things she had gone through. She talked about her relationship with God and how he helped her get through many tight spots.

Lillie was sitting there thinking, *"Oh, my God, she has gone through what I am going through right now."* Lillie was in awe to see how freely Diane talked to her about her relationship with God. She had always admired when people had no reservations talking about God anywhere and to anyone. Lillie was just starting to build her relationship with God.

Diane was not ashamed to talk about God. However, she finally stopped talking long enough to take a breath and say, "Lillie, I never pass up the opportunity to ask those who are placed in front of me whether they know God?" Diane stared Lillie right in the eyes as she waited for a response.

"When you were sitting at the other table, that's who you heard me talking to. I am so surprised you asked. I mean, I do not know him, know him. I intentionally talked to him for the first time a couple of days ago," Lillie said with a startled look on her face.

"So, do I understand this is all new to you?"

"Absolutely, it is!"

"Well, I must say, you are on a ride of your life," Diane said with a big smile. She leaned toward Lillie and put her hand on hers, then asked, "Have you accepted and received Jesus to be the Lord over your life?"

"I think I have," Lillie said as she fidgeted with her sleeves.

Determined to help Lillie in her time of despair, Diane said, "Let's make it a sure thing today, if you do not mind."

Lillie was beginning to feel uncomfortable with Diane's hand on top of hers in public while she was whispering. Someone may walk into the break room and get the wrong idea. Lillie kept looking towards the door to see if anyone was coming.

Diane said, "Lillie, do not be afraid. This is a time when your enemy would like for you to get up and walk away. But I would like to lead you in a word of prayer, and I want you to repeat after me."

Lillie looked around, leaned in, and whispered, "You mean right here, right now? I am uncomfortable doing this right now."

Diane gently patted her hand to calm her, "I'm not going to push you into doing anything you are not comfortable doing. We do not have to do this here, but I would like to continue our conversation, and I still want to pray for you. Will you agree to meet outside of work?" Lillie nodded in agreement.

Lillie and Diane arranged to meet for lunch at a local restaurant the next day. "As I was saying yesterday, Lillie, the enemy wants you to continue to do the things that cause you to sin. But I know you are tired of sinning, and that is why you went to God for help. There are times when he places people in our path so we can be His voice. I am the one He chose for you today, Lillie. I would like to say a prayer of salvation with you," Diane said.

"Prayer of Salvation? I am not quite sure what you mean by that," Lillie said, confused.

Diane explained, "This prayer will secure that your spirit will live with God in Heaven for eternity."

Lillie smiled, "Oh, I remember hearing them talk about something like that in church when I used to go. I do remember getting baptized."

"Baptized?" Diane said.

Lillie answered, "Yes, I remember that, but I do not remember saying a prayer of salvation."

"Okay, so do you understand enough about God right now?" Diane asked.

"Of course, I want my spirit to go where God lives after I die," Lillie said, excitedly.

Diane was very pleased that she and Lillie had decided to meet for lunch. She was grateful that Lillie decided to let Jesus be the Lord of her life. "Lillie, I will lead you in prayer, and I would like for you to repeat after me, please. '*Dear Heavenly Father, thank You for waking us to see this beautiful day. Thank You for being the head of our lives and sending Your Son Jesus to die on the cross for our sins. Thank You for the opportunity to receive Your Son as my Lord and Savior. Today, I make a conscious decision to open my heart and receive You as my Lord and Savior. I give You permission to be the driver of my life. Please forgive my sins and help me become the person You created me to be. Thank You, Holy Spirit! In Jesus Name, Amen.*"

Lillie repeated every word. When she was finished, they opened their eyes. Lillie took a deep breath as tears flowed down her cheeks. "Thank you so very much for caring enough to pray with me and help me get to this important point in my life. I feel so much better than I did yesterday."

With a big smile on her face, Diane said, "This is just the beginning, Lillie. The journey you are on now will be very rewarding. I am here to help you with this faith walk, if you are willing to let me."

"I would be delighted! I give you permission–I need all the help I can get. Diane, I have a lot to deal with in my life, and I hope you are ready to help me by showing me how to heal from my past hurts." Lillie said. Diane seemed to be a very skilled soldier for Christ, Lillie thought.

As Diane stood up to leave, she assured Lillie that she is equipped and willing to take on the challenge. "This was one of my missions today. Now that the mission has been completed, I must leave you. I am sure we will see each other soon."

Lillie was so very thankful for all Diane had done; she invited her to stay longer, but Diane had to leave for her next appointment.

That evening when Lillie arrived home with her babies, she went about her normal routine of preparing dinner, cleaning the kitchen, and bathing the children. Afterward, she put the boys to bed and sat quietly in her room. She tried to piece together all that Diane had said yesterday and today. Going over the conversations in her head, Lillie could not understand how it all happened so quickly. She was talking to God about her life. Diane happened to be in the room and came over to her table talking to Lillie about God–all of these things led to her receiving salvation. Lillie was amazed.

CHAPTER 20
CONVERSATION WITH GOD

L illie heard her name being called, *"Lillie!"* the voice said. Lillie thought she was hearing things, so she tried to ignore it.

"Lillie!" the voice said again.

She got up and began to walk around her apartment, looking to see if she was alone. There was no one else in the apartment with her. Lillie shook her head and began to sit down again. The voice called her name a third time, *"Lillie!"*

Lillie quickly remembered when she was talking to God before that she could not see him. Maybe it was Him who was calling her name. So, she decided to say, "Yes."

God began to talk to her, *"Lillie, you did not hear me talk to you before like I am talking to you now because you needed to speak with Diane. Please do not misunderstand me. I could have spoken directly to you, but I wanted to allow one of my servants to prepare you for listening to what I have to say to you,"* he said.

Lillie was so surprised that her Daddy had not forgotten her and had come back to talk. She said, "What do you mean by 'I needed to meet with Diane?'"

"You are now one of my children, and you are able to hear me. It is because you are my sheep, and I am your Shepherd. You can hear my voice now," God said.

"But I thought You were everywhere," Lillie said.

"I am God! I was there when you talked to Me in the break room. I was there when you moved with Mama Hannah and when you and Jabez had your first date. I was there when you and Diane met at lunch today. I was even there when you received My Son. My presence is everywhere. I am all-powerful and all-knowing. I want you to trust me to be your strength and guide," He said in a gentle voice.

"So, you know the first time Diane came to my table in the break room; I was uncomfortable responding to what she asked me," Lillie continued. "I am so thankful Diane was persistent in having me meet with her today. Otherwise, I would have missed out on a very important decision in my life," said Lillie.

"Not just 'important' my child, but, but the most important decision of a lifetime," God said.

Lillie was confused, so she asked, "Why is it the most important decision?"

God answered, *"Because the decision you made was an eternal decision. You only live on earth for a very short time, but the afterlife is eternal, and you need me in every moment of your life to live a life of light, joy, and peace."*

Lillie sat staring off, thinking what her Daddy had just made clear to her.

"Lillie! Lillie!"

"Okay! Okay! I'm sorry. I was just trying to process all of what has been happening. Can we go back to the original question I asked when I first started talking to You? What should I do about Jabez and our relationship?" said Lillie.

"I do not suggest you get to know him better than you know me because I am a jealous God. You should get to know Me, and I will guide you in everything you need to do." God said.

Lillie was listening very intently, but she was still confused. So, she asked, "How can I get to know you better when I cannot see you, but I am able to see Jabez? That seems backward to me."

God said, *"I do understand it is difficult for you to make sense of all of this. But I am glad you are discussing this matter with me. From the beginning of time, I instructed all who believe in me not to lean on their own understanding. What you understand and what I know is totally different. You see, Lillie, I can see your past, present, and future all at the same time. You, on the other hand, can only see your present and cannot see the next moment of your life. My warning to you is first, surrender and be forgiven. As you enter a relationship with Jabez, I must come first. Let me lead you and guide you. You will have difficulties in your relationship even when you put me first, but I will be holding your hand to walk you through them. You will have peace instead of worrying. You can bring anything to me, and I can transform it and cleanse it from the darkness. Do you understand what I am saying?"*

"Is that it, Daddy?" said Lillie. The conversation had gone long enough. Lillie felt very uncomfortable hearing that she should not put Jabez first.

He said, *"I can only give you small bits of information at a time; I do not want to overwhelm you. One thing you must always remember is not to put anyone or anything before Me, including Jabez. I am a very jealous God. So, you must always remember this commandment."*

Lillie listened to everything God said to her. Then, she got ready for bed after a seemingly very long and eventful day.

CHAPTER 21
DATE TOWARDS DESTINY

The day had finally come. Two hours before Jabez was expected to arrive, Lillie's phone rang. She was busy trying to find something special to wear for her date. She was hoping it was not him canceling. She nervously answered the phone, "Hello."

Jabez said, "I am sorry I did not get your address."

Lillie heard the first three words Jabez said and panicked. She murmured something under her breath before hearing the entire sentence. Lillie apologized and gave him her address.

"I will see you soon, okay?" he said.

"Okay," she said and hung up the phone.

Getting her wardrobe together seemed so difficult now when it had never been before? Lillie really wanted to look special for Jabez. He seemed to be one who liked to see her dressed up. She sensed he had a caring and kind spirit. She really wanted to impress him on their first date. Lillie had never experienced this type of feeling in her prior relationships so, working hard to have a special night was important.

Lillie had already arranged for a sitter and cleaned her apartment. So, the only thing she had to do was make sure she looked presentable. Time was moving, but it seemed as though it was moving too slow. Usually, time was moving too fast. Lillie had to stop and ask herself, *"Why am I so nervous? This is not my first time being with a man. For Heaven's sake, I have two children. Breath, Lillie, it will be okay!"*

The decision on how to fix her hair became a chore. She combed it forward, flipped it to one side, and then to the other. The clock was ticking, so she pulled the back of her hair up and fixed her bangs. As she was spraying her cologne on, the doorbell rang.

Once again, she said, *"Breath, Lillie, it will be okay!"*

Lillie heard more than one set of footsteps on the stairs leading to her apartment. She also heard voices. The closer they got to her door, the more nervous she became. Lillie's apartment was on the second floor, so when they came to the landing, someone knocked on the door. Her stomach dropped, then she paused, not moving, and took another deep breath. It had been weeks since she last saw Jabez. Lillie had no idea who was with him; it all seemed like a dream. For a moment, she had not realized she was still standing in one place and had answered the door. He knocked a second time. Lillie quickly went to the door. Lillie put her hand on the knob, unlocked the door, and stepped back as she slowly opened it. Jabez was looking totally different than she remembered. He looked extremely handsome and smelled oh so Heavenly. He had flowers and a bottle of champagne. Lillie had never had a man bring her flowers or a bottle of champagne before. Although she had two children, she could not believe this was her first "real" date. She thought, *"Wow! Jabez did all this for me."*

Lillie welcomed Jabez and his friend and told them to come in and take a seat. They continued standing as if they did not hear her. Jabez introduced his friend to her.

"What time should I come back to pick you up?" his friend asked.

Lillie was kind of shocked that he had to get a ride to her apartment on their first date. However, she thought it was a good thing they were not going out. She thought they should have discussed this before they came up to her apartment. The two of them were standing there looking at each other and making hand gestures.

Lillie could see them in her peripheral vision. She thought they were quite comical, as she pretended to ignore them. Then Lillie intervened and said, "After our date, I can take him where he needs to go." A sigh of relief came over both. The two friends shook hands and said goodbye.

Lillie and Jabez were alone in her apartment. This setting was different for them; usually, there would be others around or something to distract Lillie from holding a conversation. He was still standing with the flowers and champagne in his hand. She was standing as if she was in another world.

Jabez said, "Okay, what would you like for me to do with the flowers and champagne?"

Lillie reeled herself back into reality, apologized for daydreaming, and said, "Excuse me, I'll take them."

"If you give me the vase to put the flowers in, I can arrange them for you," Jabez said.

She had never experienced the nice little things he was offering to do.

"Well, I can do it, if you like," Lillie said.

"No, I will do it, simply because I want to celebrate you completing your training. That was a big accomplishment," said Jabez.

The six weeks of training Lillie had gone through did not seem like much to her, but she was proud of herself. It was nice having someone celebrate her. So, she went ahead and let him arrange the flowers.

"Do you mind putting the champagne in the refrigerator so it can get chilled?"

"Sure," she said.

Lillie had prepared snacks, so they sat at the kitchen table and began to eat and share stories about themselves. They did not ignore each other like they did when they first met and were riding on the bus. Lillie was nervous about this date because she found herself thinking back to the time when they were both shy and weren't talking. But now, their conversation flowed so easily, and both seemed to be comfortable with each other.

"Before we go any further, I personally want to give you accolades for a job well done and staying focused to finish what you set out to do for yourself. I can see you are a hard worker and pay attention to details. You put time into how you look, and you are very beautiful because of it. I sense you are ambitious. Let me ask you a question," Jabez said.

As Lillie was sitting soaking all of what Jabez was saying in, she was also blushing. "Before you ask me that question, will you give me time to thank you for the compliments?"

"Sure, I'm sorry. Go right ahead."

"Thank you for the compliments." They both laughed. "I want you to know you were part of the reason I completed school, as crazy as that may sound. After we were introduced, I was excited about going to school because I thought we could talk and get to know each other better. The six weeks flew by so quickly, but each day was interesting. Now you can ask your question?"

"I see you were very determined to finish the course. You went after the certificate as if it was a degree. I would like to know what your goals are in life?"

This was another thing she had never been asked before by a man. Lillie told him she wanted to be an independent woman and did not want assistance from the government. She wanted to become a wealthy entrepreneur. The one thing all of her parents taught was to work hard for what you want, and God will give you all your needs and some of your wants.

Jabez was very impressed with her answer. He saw how well she cared for her children, kept herself looking nice, her apartment was clean and organized, and she seemed to focus on her goals.

"Now it's my turn to ask questions. What was your life like as a child?" For some reason, Lillie thought he was going to say something similar to the way her childhood life was.

But when Jabez started off with, "You had to ask me that question first, didn't you?" As he started to share with her, he leaned forward and said, "See, I am from the west side of Chicago, and I grew up with rats and roaches in the ghetto." He had barely started sharing with her, and already she felt sad for him because she thought her life growing up was bad, but it was nothing compared to his. Lillie had to interrupt him on several occasions so she could get a good understanding. Jabez was surprised she had not experienced or heard some of the things he was sharing. Their conversation went on for hours. After talking so much, Jabez wanted something to drink.

"Do you mind if I get the champagne and you get the glasses?"

"Okay?"

As Lillie was getting up from the table, Jabez extended his hand to help her up. Lillie smiled and thanked him. It was very different having a man be so kind to her, but it felt like how a relationship should be. It was surprising to be involved in such a pleasant conversation, especially because they were both enjoying themselves. Lillie got the glasses, and Jabez grabbed the champagne. He slowly opened the bottle and waited a moment before pouring the champagne into the glasses.

Lillie did not understand why Jabez didn't pour the champagne right away. She laughed, "What are you doing? Why don't you just pour it?"

Jabez explained, "If I open the bottle too soon, the bubbles will overflow and make a big mess. So, I make sure all the bubbles are gone from the top of the bottle before opening it completely and pouring it." He poured them both a glass of champagne, then put the top on. Lillie invited him to sit in the living room. Jabez perked up when he noticed Lillie's music collection. He looked through the records and commented that she had a nice selection. He asked if he could play something. Lillie nodded. So, he put on a record and started singing along with the artists. He was so into each song he played. He was not shy. He closed his eyes as he sang each song. He had a very nice voice as he danced and sang as if he were performing on stage.

Lillie sat looking at him and listening to every word he sang. She was mesmerized by Jabez. When each new song started playing, he would ask if she knew who the artist was. She knew a few, but not nearly as many as he did. It was almost like a game they were playing. To have fun, she would take a guess, even when she knew it was the wrong answer. They laughed when she guessed incorrectly. He talked and sang the whole date.

While Jabez was singing his heart out, Lillie was thinking over and over what God had told her about the relationship. "Put Me first, not Jabez." He told her if she did not put Him first, things would not turn out the way she hoped. But Lillie was not listening to the advice God had given her. She told God she needed help. He tried to help by warning her–but Lillie ignored all the warnings.

Lillie felt her and Jabez's relationship was blossoming in a way neither thought it would. They were seeing each other almost every day. A few months later, Jabez moved in with Lillie and the children. Lillie knew all along her living arrangement was against God's commandments. Her pastor preached about the same thing at church. Mama Hannah and Daddy Matthew tried to talk to Lillie about not living with a man before she was married. They told her it was against God's will and often reminded her she was living in sin. Lillie began to feel ashamed about Jabez living with her. She did not want to face her parents or her pastor Sunday after Sunday. So, she stopped going to church. It was a very difficult decision because Lillie really enjoyed church. She enjoyed praising and worshipping God. When Sunday would come, her and Jabez would find something else to do to occupy their time.

Chapter 22
Hidden Truth

❧

At work, Lillie tried avoiding Diane. Before she was in a relationship with Jabez, her and Diane would see each other often. Now, anytime they ran into each other, Diane would try to strike up a conversation. However, Lillie would avoid discussing anything personal. She did not want Diane bringing up the topic about God, because she did not want to feel guilty about her life with Jabez.

Diane knew it was just a matter of time before Lilly's life fell apart because she was not being obedient to God. The road Lillie was traveling on would bring her nothing but trouble. One afternoon, Diane came into the break room and saw Lillie sitting at the table. It had been a while since they had last seen each other. Lillie did not seem to be feeling well. Diane asked, "How are you and the children doing?"

"Fine."

"Lillie are you sure? Diane asked. "You don't look fine?"

Lillie looked at Diane strangely. *"How does she know something is wrong?"* It seems as though she can sense when something is not right in people's lives. Lillie was not feeling good that she had gone against what God had warned her not to do. She had put Jabez before Him. Lillie was unnerved knowing God's eyes were watching her constantly. "Really, I'm fine," Lillie said again.

As time went on, Lillie couldn't live with her deception any longer. She finally told Jabez what God had said to her.

"I agree with God," Jabez said. "You should be putting Him first—we should both be putting Him first. I have always believed in God and have had a relationship with him since I was young. I'm not sure why I haven't spoken to you about this before."

Lillie was astonished at Jabez's response, because he had seldom mentioned anything about God. All this time Lillie had not mentioned God to Jabez, either, because she was not sure how he would respond. Now she felt silly. Lillie excused herself and went into the bathroom. There, she cried out to God, because she had been avoiding what he had told her to do for far too long. Then she surrendered to God and asked to be forgiven for not obeying Him.

Jabez sat in the living room with his head in his hands and began to confess to the Lord about his shortcomings. He knew Lillie was right. They both should have put God first in their lives. He felt bad about the poor decisions he had made with leaving God out of his life.

Neither of them realized that God could take their mistakes and use it for their own good. Having doubts and self-pity, brought about selfishness. Each of them cried out to God. This was the beginning of their healing. Opening their mouths and speaking what the Spirit of God had given them to say caused a light to begin to shine bright within them.

"Since we have cried out to the Lord separately, Lillie, will you pray with me?" Jabez said.

"Jabez, we should not be together! I do not want to continue to disappoint God," Lillie said.

"I know, but there is nothing wrong with us praying together. This is what God would want us to do. Where there are two or more gathered, Jesus will be with us." Lillie turned away from Jabez. He put his hands on her shoulders. "Lillie, just this one time. Please, pray with me! Or I will pray, if that would make you feel better." She turned to face him and nodded in agreement. Jabez took her hands in his, and they bowed their heads.

"Father in Heaven, we come to say we are sorry for not putting you first in our relationship. Please forgive us for our sins of disobedience. We know your ways lead to a safe place for those of us who follow your commandments. We sincerely want to be in your will. With you guiding our lives, we are saved from destruction. Lillie and I want to do what is right. Lead us along the path you have planned for us. In your Mighty and Powerful Son's Name, Jesus, I pray, Amen." When Jabez finished the prayer, they hugged.

"I feel so much better," Lillie said.

"So do I, and I knew we would. That is why I pleaded with you to let me pray for us. Lillie, I want to remain in our relationship, but as of tonight, I will be looking for a better paying job and my own apartment. I know this is the right thing to do," said Jabez.

"I agree! Then I will not have to feel so ashamed of you living with me."

The next morning Jabez started looking for a job. He was determined to find one. It took a couple of months for him to get hired, but he was really excited. He knew he was on the right track to making things right between him and Lillie. After saving up a few paychecks, Jabez found an apartment.

Lillie and Jabez's relationship continued to blossom. They continued talking on the phone and spending time together every day. One evening, Jabez called Lillie and told her he needed to stop by to talk to her. He told her he would come by later this evening.

That evening, when Jabez came by, Lillie noticed he was not his cheerful self. He seemed quiet as if something was bothering him. He sat on the couch in the living room, appearing to gather his thoughts. Lillie looked at him puzzled. Finally, Jabez spoke up. He told Lillie he had something real important to talk with her about.

"Lillie, remember the time we prayed together? Well, God has been nudging me to share some important information with you."

"What is it Jabez?"

"I have been wanting to tell you before now, but I was trying to decide when it would be best."

"Okay, spit it out Jabez! Don't keep me waiting! Tell me what's so important."

He rubbed his palms together and wiped sweat from his forehead. "I have a family, with three children and a wife."

"Wow! Stop, Jabez! What was that?" she said as she held her hand up in front of her. "Did I hear you say wife? You mean to tell me..."

"Please let me finish! I am in the middle of a divorce."

Lillie quickly stood and walked back and forth with her hands on her hips. "Let me wrap my head around what you just said," Lillie said waving her hands in the air. "You have a wife and three children? When were you going to tell me this important news? Come on, Jabez how could you get me twisted up in something like this? You are taking me way back to my childhood. If we continue with this love affair, we can end up with a blended family too? The two of us and our children, all under one roof. I cannot believe what I am hearing. What am I going to do with this information, God?" she said looking up.

Jabez told Lillie, "I knew you were not going to receive this information well. That is why I contemplated not telling you. Each time I thought about it, the fear of losing you as my future wife was too much to bear—and I did not want that to happen.

Jabez stood up, approached Lillie, and put his arms around her, hugging her tight. Then he rested his chin on her head and said, "I'm so sorry, so sorry. I did not mean to hurt you. I should have told you a long time ago. I just did not want to lose you." Tears started flowing from both of their eyes. They were in the midst of a turmoil, where neither of them wanted to be. Even though the news seemed to be unbearable, they hoped it would bring them closer.

They were in prayer every day talking to God about how to move beyond their brokenness. Their love for one another outweighed the sins of their past. They knew with help from God, and doing what is right, could please him. God had made a promise that their lives would turn out better than what the Devil had planned for them. God was with them through it all.

The following year, Jabez's divorce was finalized. He was given full custody of his children. He always knew after meeting Lillie and seeing how she carried herself and took care of her children, he wanted her to be his wife. He could see God's hand in their relationship. One blessing followed the other.

One day after Jabez got off work, he and Lillie met for dinner. He was as nervous as he was when they first met because he wasn't sure how she would respond to what he had to say. "Lillie, I want you to be my wife and the mother to my children."

Lillie almost choked on her water. "Jabez, why do you do things like that?"

"What do you mean? I am tired of trying to do things my way. When God prompts me to say something, I am not going to miss out on any more blessings. I think if you say, yes, this will be one of the happiest days of my life."

"I want to wait, because I do not want to be in the same situation Mama Hannah and Mama Victoria were in."

"What do you mean by that?"

"Once they got married, they had to deal with hurt, pain, rejection, and total dysfunction.

"I was in a dysfunctional marriage. So, I know what kind of hurt and pain that can cause. I will not put you through that. I want a wholesome, blended family. With God on our side, I believe it can happen."

"Okay, but let's not rush it! I am still working through the trauma it caused in my childhood."

"I want you to know I will keep asking until you say, 'Yes!'"

The marriage question came up frequently, but Lillie did not believe Jabez was serious because she was still thinking of Daddy Bubba's actions toward Mama Hannah and Mama Victoria. She did not understand the benefits of being married and was fearful of the chaos that might happen in her home. This kept her from telling Jabez that she was ready to marry him.

Lillie and Jabez started living together as a family with their five children, Lillie's two sons and Jabez's daughter and two sons. They felt they were spending too much money paying for two apartments and cooking separate meals for their two families. They told their parents they had to live together to save money. The heaviness of this decision to live together and not be married weighed on them heavily, convicting them in the eyes of the Lord. They wanted to obey God, regardless of what was going on in their lives. Pleasing God was more important to them. So Jabez knew he had to do the right thing.

"Lillie will you marry me?" asked Jabez.

Lillie said, "Yes, Jabez!"

It took him by surprise that Lillie finally agreed to marry him They had a small wedding at the church. All the children were there, along with some friends, and their families. The reception was held at their home with food, music, and entertainment. That evening they became one big, happy, blended family in the eyesight of God.

"Should your children start calling me Mama Lillie and you Daddy Jabez?" Lillie asked.

"Let's let them decide what they want to call us. He told the children to come to the table. They quickly came and sat down. "As of today, Lillie is my wife, and I am her husband. What would you all like to call us?"

They looked at each other and laughed. They talked among themselves for just a few minutes. It was a unanimous decision. "Lillie is Mama and Jabez is Daddy," they said laughing.

Then Jabez announced, "This Sunday we all will start going to church every Sunday. We will be going because God told us to. We are two families joined together as one, and we will love one another as one. Does everyone agree with that?"

"Yes!" they all shouted

Jabez and Lillie looked at each other and smiled. They knew they were doing what God had told them to do. They were looking forward to living life as a blended family who loved and served the Lord.

CHAPTER 23
THE HEALING PROCESS

B oth generations of the entire family were carrying grief, pain, and guilt in their hearts and minds. They all had a lot of burdens they were bearing in their individual situations. God's presence could help them get out of the rut they were in and transform them to a place of healing. He knew there were kings and queens inside each of them. He wanted to help bring those images out to use them for His own purpose, once they surrendered to Him and asked to be forgiven. Then, God, only God, can reposition each of them for greatness.

If you need healing, the first thing you need to do is to go to God in prayer. He is a God who will always answer. However, His answer may be yes, no, or wait. You can ask for strength and courage to help you wait on the Lord.

"He heals the brokenhearted and binds up their wounds," Psalms 147:3.

CHAPTER 24
SEEKING GOD FOR
FORGIVENESS

❧

hen we have sinned, whether we are aware of it or
not, we must ask God for forgiveness. Forgiveness
is spiritual, we cannot do it ourselves. God is the
only One who can forgive us. In this story each family member
had to admit in their own heart they had sinned and needed to
be forgiven. For one to receive forgiveness from another, he or
she must forgive others who have sinned against them. Only
then will we be forgiven. The Bible says, "For if you forgive
other people when they sin against you, your heavenly Father
will also forgive you," Matthew 6:14. God does not want us to
ask him for forgiveness, if we are not willing to forgive others.
When we ask God for forgiveness, we must take in considera-
tion that we may owe others forgiveness. Asking for what we
are not willing to give, is not of God. "Be kind and compassionate to one another, forgiving each other, just as in Christ God
forgave you" (Ephesians 4:32). God will give us plenty of opportunities to do so. Our brain is the hard drive of our body
and we do not forget what was said or done to us. The hurt is
in the hard drive, so forgiveness is not about forgetting about

what happened to you; it is about surrendering your pain and hurt to God.

Offering forgiveness to someone who comes to you asking for forgiveness for the wrong they have done against you, it can begin the healing process, releasing you and them from the bitterness and pain that we tend to cling to when we have been hurt. Be aware that everyone who does you wrong will not ask for your forgiveness, but we need to forgive them anyway because the Bible says we must.

Unforgiveness will keep you imprisoned, with anger, fear, or shame. Know that God through His Son and Holy Spirit can release you when you surrender and seek His help. He will empower you to begin the process of being healed and set free from the strongholds of life.

It is in the surrender and forgiveness that God shows up for you. It is in the surrender and forgiveness that He gives grace. It is in the surrender and forgiveness that he gives favor. It is in the surrender and forgiveness that Jesus' blood washes over you. It is in the surrender and forgiveness that you can get your breakthrough. If there is no surrendering or forgiving, you are not fully walking in your purpose. You are just existing.

I encourage you to follow the obedience of the Jabez and Lillie in this story. There are no regrets from doing what you are told by the One who sees all and knows all. He sees much more than what we do; He sees our sadness, our struggles, our delights, and our love for one another.

God bless your journey!

SCRIPTURE REFERENCES

God can use your mistakes for your good-Romans 8:28 Amplified Version (AMP).

"And we know with great confidence that God who is deeply concerned about us causes all things to work together as a plan for good for those who love God, to those who are called according to His plan and purpose."

Seek God first in all of your situations-Matthew 6:33 New International Version (NIV).

"But seek first his kingdom and his righteousness, and all these things will be given to you as well."

When you are overwhelmed with the problems of life-Matthew 11:28 NIV.

"Come to me, all you who are weary and burdened, and I will give you rest."

We all have sinned. It's important to confess your sins to God- 1 John 1:9 NIV.

"If we confess our sins, he is faithful and just and will forgive us our sins and purify us from all unrighteousness."

To be forgiven, you must forgive anyone who has offended you-Ephesians 4:32 NIV.

"Be kind and compassionate to one another, forgiving each other, just as in Christ God forgave you."

In the Bible, God says, "Do not fear" or "Fear Not" 365 times- Isaiah 41:10 AMP.

"Do not fear anything, for I am with you; Do not be afraid, for I am your God. I will strengthen you, be assured I will help you; I will certainly take hold of you with My righteous right hand, a hand of justice, of power, of victory, of salvation."

When you pray, you must believe that God hears you-Hebrews 11:6 NIV.

"And without faith it is impossible to please God, because anyone who comes to him must believe that he exists and that he rewards those who earnestly seek him."

Resources For Purify This House

The Following Books Can Be Purchased on Amazon.com:

Any Bible-Recommend New International Reader's Version

A Spiritual Marriage Versus a Secular Relationship by Willie & Althea P. Jones

Pillow Talk: Miracles (Steps in the Garden of Intimacy with God) by Sheri Hauser

Slipping Through the Cracks: Intervention Strategies for Clients with Multiple Addictions and Disorders by Mark Sanders

The Five Love Languages: How to Express Heartfelt Commitment to Your Mate by Gary Chapman, PhD

Websites

www.blendedandblack.com

www.meetup.com

www.aa.org (Alcoholics Anonymous)

www.MentalHealth.gov

For Substance Abuse and Mental Health

Substance Abuse and Mental Health Services Administration (SAMHSA) National Helpline-A free, confidential, 24/7, 365-day-a-year treatment referral and information service available in English and Spanish. **Please call 800-662-HELP (4357).**

A Children's Book by Althea P. Jones:

Joy-The Car that went Bump Ditty Bump by Althea P. Jones

BIOGRAPHY

Althea P. Jones is a writer, teacher, speaker, and life coach. She was born in a small town 130 miles south of Chicago. She currently resides in Las Vegas, NV. Althea has lived through three blended families, as a child and wife. The Holy Spirit inspired her to write this book based on her experiences to help other blended families.

Althea has been married to Willie L. Jones for 35 plus years. They have five adult children. She enjoys sharing the wisdom she has gained through her lifetime of experiences, recognizing that the trials she endured has enabled her to become better equipped to mentor others.

Althea is currently a Chaplain and Mentor for the Clark and Nye County Detention Centers for adults and teens in Las Vegas and Pahrump, Nevada. She has always had a passion for serving youth.

Althea attributes her wisdom to her relationship with God, declaring, "God saved, healed, and renewed my mind, body and soul." She has counseled people to use the tools that help transform their lives. She believes God spoke to her saying, "Now is the season for you to share your gift of writing with other blended families as well as youth."

Althea and her husband, Willie Jones, are the co-authors of two books, "*A Spiritual Marriage Versus A Secular Relationship*" and "*Joy-The Car that went Bump Ditty Bump.*"

Living life on purpose is her motto.

Shambé Jones was born in Champaign-Urbana, Illinois, where he started his creative journey at the age of five. He grew up in a family of artists, musicians, seamstresses, carpenters, farmers, etc. He attended Jackson State University, where he earned a B.A. in Fine Arts and participated in their study abroad program in Côte D'lvorie, Africa. There he studied various forms of craftwork such as weaving, sculpting, and brass casting. The people of Côte D'lvorie inspired Shambé to teach himself the art form of pyrography. He is also known for his work in painting, sculpture, ceramics, and mixed media.

Graphic Artist, Mary Williams-Cochran a native of Simi Valley California. Currently resides in Las Vegas Nevada. Mary is a gifted self-taught artist! Drawing and painting has always been a part of her life. She is an inspiring Free Lance Artist and Graphic Art Designer with her own style of creativity. She spent a few years as a military spouse, before taking up permanent residency in Las Vegas, NV. Her two amazing daughters are ages 23 and 15.

www.ingramcontent.com/pod-product-compliance
Lightning Source LLC
Chambersburg PA
CBHW051829090426
42736CB00011B/1715